CREATING 'CHURCH' AT HOME

For older people living with dementia

Patrick Coghlan

kevin
mayhew

kevin
mayhew

First published in Great Britain in 2016 by Kevin Mayhew Ltd
Buxhall, Stowmarket, Suffolk IP14 3BW
Tel: +44 (0) 1449 737978 Fax: +44 (0) 1449 737834
E-mail: info@kevinmayhew.com

www.kevinmayhew.com

9 8 7 6 5 4 3 2 1 0

ISBN 978 1 84867 840 8
Catalogue No. 1501517

Cover design by Rob Mortonson
© Image used under licence from Shutterstock Inc.
Edited by Nicki Copeland
Typeset by Angela Selfe
Proofread by Virginia Rounding

Printed and bound in Great Britain

Contents

About the author

Patrick is Minister at Worstead Baptist Church in Meeting Hill (North Norfolk). He is a trustee and chaplain of Aylsham and district Care Trust (ACT), and manager of 4C's Aylsham Counselling Centre. ACT is a Christian community care charity, which is part of the St Michael's Care Complex in Aylsham, and the organisation does a lot of work with older people.

In his work as a minister, chaplain and counsellor, Patrick has had considerable experience of working with people of most age groups, in the context of providing ministry and care – many of whom have been quite vulnerable – including those living with varying types and degrees of dementia.

Patrick is married to June and they have two grown-up children – Rachel and Jonathan. For his leisure Patrick enjoys quality family time, walking the two family dogs and riding his red motorcycle.

Patrick has been an enthusiastic author for many years, having had his first book published in 2001. He has written a variety of Christian resources for different age groups, and some family novels.

Introduction

After many years of involvement in a church fellowship – experiencing the spiritual input, support, encouragement, love and friendships it offers – a huge void must be left in people's lives when that is no longer possible, as a result of difficult or changing circumstances. I have written *Creating 'church' at home* with that in mind. My intention was to produce some ideas and material to enable an act of worship to take place in the home – even for those with no ministerial or leadership experience – and for it to be done in such a way that it would be deep and meaningful.

Creating 'church' at home is focused towards older people who are living with dementia, who may struggle to cope with a full-length service or Bible study. *Creating 'church' at home* can be used as a personal resource or may be enjoyed with one or two carers, friends, neighbours or family members. It is a user-friendly, off-the-page, Bible-based resource that has the flexibility of being adapted to different situations. More about that in the following chapters.

The approach taken by *Creating 'church' at home* is to build up an understanding of the individual who is living with dementia – which may be yourself – as that will form the basis of the approach to the act of worship. This includes the style of the time of spiritual preparation leading into the act of worship and the way the room is set up for the occasion (in a way that is familiar, comfortable and meaningful).

There are two different contexts in which to use *Creating 'church' at home* (by using the two different options in the worship sessions). These are described in detail in the following two chapters.

Living with dementia
Carer for someone who is living with dementia

N.B. Using the short messages from the author (see 'How to use this book'), pick out which of these two chapters best describes your situation. Turn to the appropriate page: you only need to read that one chapter before beginning your preparations for the 25 ministry sessions that follow.

How to use this book

Using the short messages from the author (below), pick out which of the following best describes your situation. You only need to read that one chapter before beginning your preparations for the 25 ministry sessions that follow.

- You are living with the early stages of dementia and are finding it too tiring, stressful or difficult to attend and participate in church activities on a regular basis. If this describes your situation, and you want to enjoy a fulfilling act of worship at home, then chapter 1 is for you.

- You are caring for someone (or are a good friend, neighbour or family member of someone) who is living with dementia and finds it too tiring, stressful or difficult to attend and participate in church activities on a regular basis. If this describes your situation, and you want to organise worship sessions for them at home, then chapter 2 is for you.

CHAPTER ONE

Living with dementia

You are living with the early stages of dementia and are finding it too tiring, stressful or difficult to attend and participate in church activities on a regular basis. If this describes your situation, and you want to enjoy a fulfilling act of worship at home, then this chapter is for you.

Getting to know you

Living with dementia, you could be finding it more difficult to understand and connect with acts of public worship and Bible study. If your faith and involvement in the Church has been a large part of your life (maybe for many years), you may be struggling at times to find sufficient spiritual nourishment. But perhaps more than that, you could be finding it difficult to fully enter into worshipping God on your own. Maybe you dream that 'church' could be brought into your home and personalised to your situation.

We know that the Church is the people and not the building or its furnishings; however, it could be helpful to you to reproduce some of those elements that have been a part of your worship over the years – in your own home: those things that are familiar, comforting and helpful to your worship; things that will assist in making your worship experience personal; and things that will help you to connect with God and have a truly fulfilling worship experience.

The intention of *Creating 'church' at home* is to endeavour to help you to replicate at least something of the church experience that you have been used to and have treasured – in order to help you to achieve a satisfying spiritual life. Feelings are very important to those living with dementia, and it is hoped that this resource will help to re-create some of your feelings connected with the act of worshipping God.

Consider carefully your own church background and preferences. Think about the following questions. You may want to discuss this with a friend or family member. The conclusions you arrive at will be the basis of how you could set the scene for your personal worship sessions (using the resources provided in *Creating 'church' at home*).

- What denomination have you been used to?
- Do you like a formal or an informal approach to worship?
- Is your preference for a modern or a more traditional style?
- How was the building in which you used to worship laid out?
- What are your favourite hymns, and what is your preferred style of church music?
- What is your preferred version of the Bible?
- Did you have a particular role in the church: for example, musician, choir member or worship leader, lay reader or local preacher, Sunday school teacher, flower arranger, etc.?

Setting the scene

Spend some time – or ask a friend, neighbour or family member to help – collecting together some resources which will help to replicate something of the style and feeling of the place and situation where you have been used to worshipping in the past.

- Take your Bible readings from the version of the Bible that you prefer.

- If you have been used to having symbols like a cross, some candles or a banner to focus on at the front, get a small, free-standing cross, some candles (battery ones are probably safer in the home), a banner, etc. to re-create the feel of what you have been used to.

- You might like to brighten up the room with some flowers or a flowering plant, placed somewhere prominent.

- You may already have some CDs of the kind of church music that you like and feel comfortable with: have one playing quietly in the background at the beginning of your worship session.

- If you were a church musician and you have an instrument and are still able to play, you might like to provide the music yourself.

- If you were in the choir, a worship leader or an enthusiastic singer, you might like to join in and sing with the CD.

- If you were involved in a teaching ministry, I am sure you can add your mark to the sessions in some way.

- It is your time and setting: do with it exactly as you would like.

Guide to using the material

- Set out the room – including the music playing quietly in the background.

- **Be still and quiet:** Spend some time being still and quiet in God's presence, listening to the background music which is playing, in preparation for using the resources provided for your act of personal worship. Focus on the theme during this time.

- **Passage to read:** The Bible references for a psalm or part of a psalm to read. Read it out loud if you prefer.

- Select **(Option1) To do:** This involves making a choice which is linked with or in some way leads into the theme.

- **Story to tell (in the author's words):** Read this familiar Bible story (out loud if preferred), which is told in the author's own words (Bible references are given). The author endeavours to bring out a spiritual message at the end of the retelling of the story, as indicated by the subheading.

- **Prayer of response and the Lord's Prayer:** Draw the session to a close in a positive way. (The bracketed words are either allowing for additional material or, in most cases, for use in a shared worship session.)

- **Be still and quiet:** If you would like to, spend some more time in God's presence in an attitude of worship as you listen to the CD again (or sing or play some more music yourself).

CHAPTER TWO

Carer for someone who is living with dementia

You are caring for someone (or are a good friend, neighbour or family member of someone) who is living with dementia and finds it too tiring, stressful or difficult to attend and participate in church activities on a regular basis. If this describes your situation, and you want to organise worship sessions for them at home, then this chapter is for you.

You can make a big difference

If you have a positive attitude, it will help you to have a positive approach in organising and participating in these worship sessions with the person you are caring for (good friend to, neighbour of, or a family member of) who is living with dementia. Hopefully that will help these sessions to be uplifting and enriching times of worship, and to reinforce feelings of inner peace and joy.

By taking the trouble to find out more about the person, and having the attitude that it is about living with dementia and not dying from it, you can make a real difference to that person's quality of life – in a good way.

Getting to know the person

People living with dementia still have spiritual needs. This is highlighted if they have a strong faith and have been actively involved in the Church in the past (maybe for many years).

Try to imagine the frustration of no longer being able to attend or fully engage in public worship, group Bible studies or sharing fellowship with Christians in other ways. You have picked up this resource on behalf of someone who is in that position.

We know that the Church is the people and not the building or its furnishings; however, it could be helpful to that person living with dementia to reproduce some of those elements that have been part of their worship over the years – in their home: those things that are familiar, comforting and helpful to their worship; things that will assist in making their worship personal; and things that will help them to connect with God and have a truly fulfilling worship experience.

The intention of *Creating 'church' at home* is to endeavour to help you to replicate at least something of the church experience that the recipient has been used to and has treasured, as you draw alongside them to help them to find satisfaction in their spiritual life.

You are a carer, a good friend, a neighbour or a family member of the recipient. I would encourage you to find out as much about the church background and preferences of that person as you can, in order to make their worship experience really count. Talk about the following questions with the recipient, and maybe (with their permission) chat with their minister. The conclusions you arrive at will form the basis of how you could set the scene for your shared worship sessions (using the worship material provided in *Creating 'church' at home*).

- What denomination has the recipient been used to?

- Does the recipient like a formal or an informal approach to worship?

- Is the recipient's preference for a modern or a more traditional style?

- How was the building in which the recipient's worship took place laid out?

- What are the recipient's favourite hymns, and what is their preferred style of church music?

- What is the recipient's preferred version of the Bible?

- Did the recipient have a particular role in the church: for example, musician, choir member or worship leader, lay reader or local preacher, Sunday school teacher, flower arranger, etc.?

Setting the scene

Spend some time collecting together some resources which will help you to replicate something of the style and feelings of the place and situation where the recipient has been used to worshipping in the past. The recipient themselves may like to help with this process.

- Take the Bible readings from the version of the Bible that the recipient prefers.

- If the recipient has been used to having symbols like a cross, some candles or a banner to focus on at the front, get a small, free-standing cross, some candles (battery ones are probably safer in the home), a banner, etc. to re-create the feel of what they have been used to.

- You might like to brighten up the room with some flowers or a flowering plant, placed somewhere prominent.

- The recipient may already have some CDs of the kind of church music that they like and feel comfortable with: have one playing quietly in the background at the beginning of the worship session.

- If the recipient was a church musician and has an instrument and is still able to play, they might like to provide the music themselves.

- If the recipient was in the choir, a worship leader or an enthusiastic singer, they might like to join in and sing with the CD.

- If the recipient was involved in a teaching ministry, I am sure they can add their mark to the sessions in some way.

- It is the recipient's time and setting: do with it exactly as they would like.

Guide to using the material

- Set out the room – including the music playing quietly in the background.

- **Be still and quiet:** Spend some time sitting with the recipient being still and quiet in God's presence, listening to the background music which is playing, in preparation for using the resources provided for your act of shared worship. Try to both focus on the theme during this time.

- **Passage to read:** The Bible references for a psalm or part of a psalm to read out loud.

- Select **(Option 2)**

  - **A gentle prompt:** A suggestion for visual aids (which are linked with or in some way lead into the main theme of the session), to help stimulate memory and thoughts.

- **What do you think?** A discussion topic relevant to the visual aid.

- **Key words:** Some suggested key words that may also be used to stimulate memory and promote the discussion.

• **Story to tell (in the author's words):** Read this familiar Bible story out loud, which is told in the author's own words (Bible references are given). The author endeavours to bring out a spiritual message at the end of the retelling of the story, as indicated by the subheading.

• **Prayer of response and the Lord's Prayer:** Draw the session to a close in a positive way. (The bracketed words are either allowing for additional material or, in most cases, for use in a shared worship session.)

• **Be still and quiet:** If you or the recipient would like to, spend some more time in God's presence in an attitude of worship as you listen to the CD again (or sing or play some more music yourselves).

WORSHIP SESSIONS

PART ONE

The Church Calendar

Lent

Be still and quiet: Being prepared – Making a response to Jesus' death and resurrection.

Passage to read: Psalm 15.

(Option 1)
To do: Choose a favourite outfit from your wardrobe that you might wear if you were preparing to go to a wedding.

(Option 2)
A gentle prompt: Suit case, sponge bag, passport, etc.

What do you think? Talk about preparing for a holiday.

- Key words: packing, tickets, travelling, arrival and welcome.

Story to tell (in the author's words):
(Based on Matthew 25:1-13)

Jesus told this parable as a way of explaining what the kingdom of heaven would be like.

> Ten young ladies had been invited to a wedding: five were wise and five were not so wise. They arrived for the celebrations – dressed up for the occasion – only to discover that the bridegroom still hadn't arrived. It was getting quite late – and dark – so it was a good job the ladies had brought their oil lamps with them.
> There was a lot of laughter and chatter while they were sitting waiting, and the time passed quite

quickly. Indeed, it got very late, and the groom had still not arrived. At that point, some of the lamps began to flicker – a sure sign that the oil was running low. Fortunately, the five wise ladies had brought some spare oil. They hurriedly topped up their lamps, and carried on chatting. However, the five not-so-wise ladies had not come prepared.

'Can you spare us some of your oil?' they pleaded to the wiser members of the party.

'No, we can't; because then we will run short. You should have thought about this when you got ready to come!'

After a few minutes' thought, the not-so-wise ladies jumped up. 'We're just popping out to see if we can buy some more oil. Wait for us if the groom arrives while we're away.'

And the bridegroom did arrive in their absence; but there wasn't time to wait.

'Come on in, ladies, and join the celebrations,' the groom invited.

The five wise ladies who were there – prepared, ready and waiting – hurried in, before the door was firmly shut and locked behind them. The wedding banquet was laid out: it looked amazing – so much lovely food and drink. Time to party!

When the not-so-wise ladies arrived back, having bought some more oil, they banged on the door. 'Open up and let us in! Sorry we're late!'

But they were not allowed in, because they had not been prepared and ready for the arrival of the bridegroom. What a tragic end to the story!

What it means to be spiritually prepared

Jesus is talking about his return (his second coming); he is pleading with us to be spiritually prepared for that time by making a positive response to his death and resurrection – entering into a personal relationship with him. The wedding feast represents the ultimate fulfilment of the kingdom. All the young ladies represent those who profess to be followers of Jesus. Those who come prepared with spare oil represent those whose commitment of faith is evidenced by an appropriate lifestyle. Those who come unprepared represent those whose profession of faith has no real evidence in their lifestyle. The message is that only those who are truly prepared will enter into God's eternal kingdom.

As we get older, we can find ourselves thinking more about what happens after death, and whether or not we are prepared for that time. This story becomes particularly relevant if that is where you are in your life's journey.

Prayer (renewing, affirming and strengthening our relationship and daily walk with Jesus):

Lord Jesus,
as I (we) think about being prepared for Easter and the significance of the events to me (us) today, I (we) also think about being prepared for your second coming.
Fill me (us) with a sense of urgency to be ready for your return. During this period of Lent, help me (us) to look seriously at my (our) relationship with you, and to think about how your death, resurrection and ascension are relevant to me (us) today. Let this be a time of Bible study, prayer and listening to your answers.

Help me (us) to walk closer to you day by day, and to evidence my (our) faith by living out an appropriate lifestyle – living according to your teaching and example.
I (We) pray for those who are not prepared for your return. Amen.

Finish with the Lord's Prayer.

Mothering Sunday

Be still and quiet: The parenthood of God – being part of God's family.

Passage to read: Psalm 68:4-6.

(Option 1)
To do: Choose some pictures from a magazine of what would appear to be family groups.

(Option 2)
A gentle prompt: A selection of family photographs, old and recent (including a photograph of the church family, if possible).

What do you think? Talk about family members and what it means to be part of a family (including the church family).

- Key words: love, care, happiness, belonging and hugs.

Story to tell (in the author's words):
(Based on Luke 15:11-32)

You probably know this story – it must be one of the most well known of Jesus' parables – but don't worry if you're not familiar with it.

> It all started on a family farm in the countryside. A father and his two sons worked together growing crops and caring for livestock. The elder of the two sons was totally dedicated to his father and the farm, but the younger son was unsettled: he believed he

was missing out on something. And so, one day he asked his father if they could have a chat.

The loving father smiled at his son. 'What is it?'

The younger son didn't believe in beating about the bush. 'I want my money now. I want my share of what the farm is worth so that I can go out and be free – live my life!'

His father could have refused, but he knew that his son would only become more restless and rebellious. 'Come and see me tomorrow, and I will give you the value of your inheritance.'

The next day, bags packed and a wallet stuffed full of money, the young man waved goodbye to his old life, and began his journey. He believed that this was true freedom and the route to unending joy. With so much money he could travel, party, have as many girlfriends as he liked and be thoroughly extravagant. Indeed, the women flocked to him, and he was surrounded by friends – he'd never been so popular before. But what he didn't realise was how quickly the money was going. Before very long he was broke. And he got caught up in a severe famine.

'Lend some money to your old friend, just to tide me over,' he asked his so-called best mate.

'You've got to be joking. You're no friend of mine!'

A day or two later the young runaway managed to get a job on a pig farm. It was hard work, and the pay was rubbish. He felt so hungry as he thought about how well fed he had always been at home. And he missed his dad so much – and even his older brother (though they hadn't always seen eye to eye).

'I can't go home, not after letting Dad down so badly,' he told himself for several weeks – until eventually he became so desperate that he decided he would return.

It was a long way. But what the lad didn't realise was that every day since he had left home, his father had walked out to the open plains to see if he could see his lost son returning in the distance. So while the young man was rehearsing what he would say to his dad, he was spotted in the distance. Despite the heat of the day, the boy's father ran for all he was worth to meet his returning son.

'Accept me back as one of your servants, if you will . . . please,' the boy mumbled.

'Come here and give your old dad a big hug, and stop all that nonsense about being a servant,' his father said as he flung his arms around his son.

There was a big party that evening, and although the lad's older brother was a bit put out – to say the least – his father explained that he loved them both equally.

Belonging to God's family

What an amazing father! So loving, generous, welcoming, forgiving and faithful. The younger son doesn't really deserve his father's kindness. And the older son is a little self-centred about his brother's return – although maybe understandably so.

This is a story about God's amazing love for each one of us. The younger son is like us when we turn our backs on God, tempted to satisfy our self-centred desires. The older son is like us when maybe we are a little self-righteous and judgemental.

But the thing that really stands out is the amazing forgiveness that the father offers – the same forgiveness that God offers to us today!

God longs for us to be part of his heavenly family, and to experience his parenthood forever. In later life, often family takes on a far greater significance than ever before. How significant is God's family in your life?

Prayer (giving thanks for mums, asking a blessing on parents and families, and giving thanks for and asking to be included in God's heavenly family):

Heavenly Father,
thank you that whatever I (we) do, you never stop loving me (us).
Thank you that even if I (we) have turned my (our) back(s) on you to go my (our) own way, you receive me (us) back with a warm welcome and forgiveness.
Help me (us) to be willing to be part of your family.
Thank you for earthly parents – especially mums!
Be with me as a (all of us who are) parent(s), grandparent(s) or great-grandparent(s) and help me (us) in the role(s) that I (we) play.
Fill me (us) with your love to share – and give me (us) wisdom.
Thank you for my family (our families) which is (are) so important to me (us).
I (We) pray for a blessing upon all families.
In Jesus' name.
Amen.

Finish with the Lord's Prayer.

Palm Sunday

Be still and quiet: Jesus' victorious return – the victory has been won over sin and evil; share the joy and celebration.

Passage to read: Psalm 98.

(Option 1)
To do: Choose a suitable name for a 'royal' donkey. What were the reasons for your choice?

(Option 2)
A gentle prompt: A selection of sports trophies or something else symbolic of winning a victory.

What do you think? Talk about the sports trophies or other articles symbolic of winning a victory.

- Key words: victory, celebration, hope and return.

Story to tell (in the author's words):
(Based on Luke 19:28-48)

This story has to be one of the most visual stories in the New Testament, and it is a very important story for a number of reasons – so here goes!

> Jesus was fast approaching the villages of Bethphage and Bethany when he called two of his disciples over for a word. 'I have a job for you two. I want you to go ahead of us into the village to get a donkey, please.'

There were some blank looks. 'What?'

Jesus elaborated. 'When you reach the village you will see a donkey colt tied up. I want you to untie it and bring it back here to me.'

'What if someone says something to us? What should we say?'

Jesus smiled convincingly. 'Just tell them that I need it.'

It happened just as Jesus had said it would. The two disciples found the colt. The owner spotted them and asked what they thought they were doing. They gave the reply, 'The Lord needs him.' And the owner was happy with that.

'But what's it for?' The disciples asked when the two arrived back.

Jesus turned to them, smiling. 'I'm going to ride him, of course.'

So the disciples threw a couple of cloaks across the animal's back and held onto the beast while Jesus got on. 'Where are you going?'

'We are going to continue on into Jerusalem.'

As Jesus approached Jerusalem on the back of the donkey, a crowd built up and people began to spread their cloaks out on the road in front. In loud voices they shouted praises to Jesus for all the miracles they had seen him perform. In a humble way, it reflected the return of a victorious king. It was indeed a joyous occasion, but there was a sadness in Jesus' heart as he rode towards his destination. He knew that his triumphal entry would spark a great deal of resistance to him and his ministry, and would eventually lead to his death on a cross.

Once in Jerusalem, Jesus entered into the temple – as he had before. But he was horrified to see all the traders busy doing business in the temple on this occasion.

'This is supposed to be a place of prayer,' he said in a very loud voice, 'and look what you have turned it into.' With that, Jesus began to drive them out.

Every day, Jesus went into the temple, teaching those who came to listen to him. He was a very popular figure with many people, although there were those who stood in the background watching and plotting his death. But it was difficult for them to do anything when Jesus was always surrounded by crowds of people who were hanging on to every word that he said. And so those who were against Jesus (like the chief priests and teachers of the law) were biding their time very carefully.

Celebrate Jesus' victory and experience the joy

There are various things going on during what we know as Palm Sunday:

The event is confrontational to those who oppose Jesus, especially when he goes into the temple and begins to drive the traders out. There are those who begin to plot against him. So by entering into Jerusalem, Jesus understands that he is heading towards his death on the cross; but he shows his willingness to still be part of the Father's plan.

Also, importantly, it is symbolic of the triumphal entry of a king victoriously returning from the battlefield, to rule his kingdom. This predicts Jesus' second coming, victorious over sin, evil and death, when his kingdom will reach its ultimate fulfilment. For those who are followers of Jesus it will be a time of joy and celebration as we share in the victory (see Revelation 17:14)!

The adverse effects of old age in the 'here and now' do not compromise the celebration and eternal joy we will experience when Jesus returns, when, as followers of him, we will experience the kingdom in all its fullness.

Prayer (giving thanks for the promise that we as followers of Jesus will share in Jesus' victory over sin and evil, when he returns):

Lord Jesus,
thank you that though we are still in the spiritual battle, you have won the ultimate victory over sin and evil, through your death and resurrection.
Thank you that, as a result of the victory, when you return, your kingdom will reach its ultimate fulfilment, and you will rule as King.
Thank you that as a follower (as followers) of you, I (we) will share in that victory – and be part of your eternal kingdom.
Thank you that everyone has the opportunity to be there! Encourage people to choose to follow you.
Thank you for the joy and sense of celebration that is promised when you return, which not even old age can take away from us.
Amen.

Finish with the Lord's Prayer.

Maundy Thursday

Be still and quiet: 'God willing' – accepting and doing God's will.

Passage to read: Psalm 40:1-8.

(Option 1)
To do: Choose a favourite Easter hymn and read it through (either using a hymn book or from the internet). You might even know one off by heart.

(Option 2)
A gentle prompt: A notepad and a pen.

What do you think? Decide on a 'to do' list for the day ahead, and talk about what it means to say, 'God willing'.

- Key words: making plans, future, unexpected and change.

Story to tell (in the author's words):
(Based on Matthew 26:36-46)

> Jesus and his disciples were walking towards Gethsemane. There wasn't a great deal of conversation on the way after the things that had been said by Jesus earlier in the day about his death. The mood was sombre on their arrival.
>
> Jesus turned to his disciples. 'Sit down on the grass and wait for me while I go and pray.' He was

experiencing deep emotions as he took Peter, James and John further on with him. 'Keep alert while I go and pray.'

Jesus pleaded with the Father that he might be set free from the suffering and painful death that lay before him. He finished his prayer with the words, 'But it's not what I want; it is your will that should be done.'

Returning to his disciples, Jesus was disappointed that they had fallen asleep. Once again he asked them to remain alert, and this time also to join him in praying, commenting, 'I know that you have good intentions, but the body is weak.'

Jesus went away again to pray. This time he prayed that if a painful death on the cross were the only way, then so be it – finishing with the words, 'It is your will that should be done.'

On his return to the disciples Jesus found them sleeping again, so he left them, returning to pray for a third time. Once again Jesus finished his prayer with, 'It is your will that should be done.'

As Jesus walked back to where his disciples were sleeping, he had his answer from the Father: he knew exactly what he should do. 'Wake up. It's time. My betrayer is approaching.'

God's will be done

It is easy for us to fall into the trap of believing that, as Jesus approaches a terrible death on the cross, he is quite at ease about it. But that is not the case: the humanity of Jesus means that he feels the pain and the emotions that we feel – but his priority is always to do the Father's will.

There are life experiences that we struggle with. We shouldn't feel guilty if we battle with our feelings linked to those events. But we should always strive to accept the Father's will in all situations.

As we get older, time seems to go so much faster and if we are struck with health problems the immediate future can seem very uncertain; as a result we might reach the point of becoming more aware of the value of each day – a gift from God. And so the saying 'God willing' begins to have far greater significance to us.

Prayer (for the strength to live according to God's will):

Loving heavenly Father,
thank you for the gift of time. Help me (us) to value it, and grant me (us) the enablement to fit into each day those things that are important.
Thank you that your will is perfect.
Be with me (us) during those difficult and testing circumstances that I (we) will meet during my (our) life's journey: strengthen and uphold me (us).
But help me (us) to always accept and live according to your will.
I (We) pray that your will be done on earth.
In Jesus' name.
Amen.

Finish with the Lord's Prayer.

Good Friday

Be still and quiet: Jesus' death on the cross – the penalty for sin has been paid in full.

Passage to read: Psalm 67.

(Option 1)
To do: Choose one of the Ten Commandments (Exodus 20:1-17), either the one that you feel is most applicable to you or one that you struggle to obey.

(Option 2)
A gentle prompt: A selection of household bills, credit cards and a cheque book.

What do you think? Talk about the consequences of not being able to afford to pay the bills.

• Key words: bills, debt, price and paid.

Story to tell (in the author's words):
(Based on Luke 23:26-49)

> It was a long, sad procession that headed towards Calvary. A man called Simon had been forced to carry the cross that Jesus was to be crucified on. Perhaps the Romans feared that, if he were made to carry the heavy cross, Jesus might die before they reached their destination. And there were two other men, both criminals, who were led out to be crucified with Jesus. One was put to death on each side of Jesus.

We cannot even begin to imagine the pain and suffering that Jesus went through on the cross that day. The rustic nails that were driven through his hands and feet were probably hardly sharp enough to penetrate. Then there was the heat of the day, the pain, the trauma, and the ridicule . . . Every breath of air a struggle.

Apparently, onlookers divided up his clothes between them.

But Jesus looked down lovingly at those who were responsible for his death. 'Forgive them, Father.'

Soldiers offered Jesus wine vinegar and jeered at him: 'Get yourself down from there, you so-called King of the Jews!' Someone had attached a notice to the cross above Jesus' head, to that effect.

And then one of the criminals started to join in with the ridicule, 'If you really are the Messiah, you could save all three of us.'

The other criminal jumped to Jesus' defence. 'We deserve this; we are paying the penalty for our crimes, but this man has done nothing wrong.' Then he turned to Jesus. 'Remember me when you come into your kingdom.'

Jesus smiled. 'Of course. You will be with me in paradise today.'

Soon after that, Jesus cried out to the Father and died.

The price has been paid

There are three things that really stand out in this story. The first is the depth of love Jesus has for each one of us – that he is prepared to suffer and die in such a terrible way to pay the penalty for our sin. The second is the amazing faith of the criminal who asks Jesus to remember him. And the third is the instant forgiveness of that criminal and his eternal reward.

Jesus has paid the price that no one else could pay! He has made it possible for us to be forgiven and to live in his presence for eternity – surrounded by his blessing.

There is a tendency in older age to look back over the years – maybe with some regrets. Most of us are prepared to admit that sometimes we have 'got it wrong': we have made bad decisions, we have not always been entirely honest, sometimes we have been selfish, at times we have responded in thoughtless ways, and so on. It's not about feeling a failure or being a bad person; it's about reaching out for forgiveness – forgiveness so complete that our sin is as far away from us as the East is from the West (see Psalm 103:12).

Prayer (giving thanks that the penalty for sin has been paid, through Jesus' act of love on the cross):

Lord Jesus,
thank you for your amazing love for everyone, and that you died on the cross, paying the price that no one else could afford – paying the penalty for sin.
Thank you that by so doing, you have made it possible for everyone to be forgiven, and to be assured of an eternal place in your heavenly kingdom.
Help me (us) to recognise that I am (we are all) guilty of sin, as I (we) approach you in repentance and faith.
Forgive me (us) for those times that I (we) have 'got it wrong'.
Let others hear and respond to the message that the price for sin has been paid!
In your name.
Amen.

Finish with the Lord's Prayer.

Easter Sunday

Be still and quiet: Life after death – heaven.

Passage to read: Psalm 23.

(Option 1)
To do: Choose a favourite spring flower from a gardening book or magazine (or the internet).

(Option 2)
A gentle prompt: A photograph of mountains, a bottle of wine (or a soft drink) and something nice to eat (see Isaiah 25:6-8).

What do you think? Talk about going out for a really good meal.

- Key words: banquet, carvery, dessert, cake and wine.

Story to tell (in the author's words):
(Based on Luke 24:13-35)

> Their hearts were very heavy as Cleopas and his friend were walking from Jerusalem to Emmaus. The journey was about seven miles – but it seemed further! They were speaking about the traumatic events of the past few days, when suddenly a stranger joined them and began to walk with them.
>
> The stranger enquired, 'What are you talking about?'
>
> The two travellers came to a halt, turning to him in surprise. One of them questioned, 'Haven't you heard about the things that have happened?'

'What things?'

The traveller explained, 'Jesus of Nazareth has been crucified. We had hoped that he was the Messiah – what a disappointment! But then some of the women went to the tomb this morning and had a vision of angels who told them that Jesus was alive. Some of the others went to the tomb later in the day, and they confirmed what the women had said. Now we don't know what to think or believe.'

The stranger looked saddened. 'But the prophets said that the Messiah would suffer.' He went on to explain the meaning of the Scriptures concerning the Messiah as the others listened carefully.

When they arrived at Emmaus, the stranger acted as if he were going to continue on his journey. The others urged, 'It's late! Will you not stay with us tonight?'

The stranger smiled warmly. 'I appreciate that, thank you.'

During dinner, the stranger picked up a fresh loaf of bread, gave thanks to God and broke it, handing it round to everyone at the table. It was one of those moments of realisation, but at that instant in time the stranger disappeared.

'Why didn't we recognise that it was Jesus?' one of the travellers questioned in complete disbelief. 'It was so obvious!'

'There was something so special about the way he explained the Scriptures: we should have known,' the other added.

But, of course, they had been prevented from recognising Jesus until the moment he broke the bread, in the way he had done so many times before.

The two men couldn't contain their excitement. 'We have to go back to Jerusalem, right now, and tell the others that Jesus really has risen from the dead.'

A home in heaven

So what is the message of Easter Sunday? It's quite simple really: Jesus rose from the dead and is alive today. Death is not the end when we have a personal relationship with him. There is life after death, which the daffodils – associated with the springtime and Easter – have come to symbolise! And there is a heaven!

The older we get, perhaps the more significant the hope of heaven becomes – especially in times of bereavement, when we become more aware of our own mortality and seek some kind of comfort for that person who has passed away. (I appreciate, of course, that it is not just older people who meet with bereavement.)

Prayer (giving thanks for, and finding hope in the promise of eternal life):

Loving heavenly Father,
thank you that Jesus rose from the dead and is alive today.
Thank you that he has conquered death.
Thank you that through my (our) relationship with Jesus, I am (we are) assured of life after death – in heaven.
Help me (us) to hold on to that hope.
I (We) pray that others might think seriously about their eternal future.
In Jesus' name.
Amen.

Finish with the Lord's Prayer.

Ascension

Be still and quiet: Jesus will return – completing the plan and a new beginning.

Passage to read: Psalm 27.

(Option 1)
To do: Choose a small job to do around the house: for example, washing up, tidying the breakfast things, putting clean washing in the drawers or cleaning shoes. When the job is finished, feel the satisfaction associated with starting and finishing a job – big or small.

(Option 2)
A gentle prompt: Some tools of the trade (relate it to the individual's trade, profession or hobbies).

What do you think? Talk about finishing a job and then planning a new project.

- Key words: finished, pride, satisfaction and perfection (as near as can be achieved).

Story to tell (in the author's words):
(Based on Acts 1:1-11)

> Let me put a question to you: Why did Jesus make so many resurrection appearances to so many different people? Maybe you have an answer, or perhaps it's something you have never considered.

After Jesus rose from the dead, God's plan was that there would be indisputable proof that Jesus was alive; namely, that lots of people would witness the risen Jesus. And they did!

Following his resurrection but while he was still on earth, Jesus instructed his apostles, 'Stay in Jerusalem until you receive the power of the indwelling Holy Spirit. He will equip you to be my witnesses all over the world.'

Then Jesus ascended into heaven right in front of them. They watched until a cloud obscured their vision. The group of onlookers were still gazing up into the sky when they realised they had company. Two angelic beings were standing beside them – dressed in white.

'What are you looking at?' they quizzed. The group were speechless. 'Jesus will come back one day, in exactly the same way as you have seen him go into heaven.'

After completing the plan comes a new beginning

I wonder how the disciples feel after Jesus has ascended into heaven. So much has happened so quickly: Jesus' arrest, death and resurrection, and now he has left them again, to go into heaven. There must be a degree of confusion about the past and about what lies ahead.

It is always good to see a plan come together, to finish a task that has maybe taken a long time to perform. Jesus' return will mark the imminent but ultimate fulfilment of the kingdom: the bringing together of Jesus and his Church – that includes all of us who follow him.

Although Jesus' return signifies the completion of a plan, it also signifies a completely fresh and new beginning, with no more brokenness. It will be a new chapter in our lives, and in God's plan for creation.

What a wonderful thought in old age: a new beginning to look forward to!

Prayer (looking forward to the ultimate fulfilment of the kingdom):

Loving heavenly Father,
thank you that from the beginning of creation, you have had a wonderful plan that will bring prosperity and blessing.
I (We) look forward to the imminent but ultimate fulfilment of your kingdom, when Jesus returns. Only you know when that will be.
Help me (us) to be ready for that time, so that I (we) may be part of your kingdom, through my (our) relationship with Jesus.
Thank you that when your kingdom reaches its ultimate fulfilment it will not just mark the completion of the plan, but also a new beginning.
Give me (us) the boldness to speak to others about your plan.
In Jesus' name.
Amen.

Finish with the Lord's Prayer.

Pentecost

Be still and quiet: The Holy Spirit – cleansing, transforming and empowering.

Passage to read: Psalm 93.

(Option 1)
To do: Choose from a duster, vacuum cleaner, cobweb brush or broom, and then do a few minutes of dusting, vacuuming, cleaning down cobwebs or sweeping a floor, as appropriate.

(Option 2)
A gentle prompt: A selection of dusters, brushes, etc.

What do you think? Talk about cleaning the house, knocking cobwebs down out of the corners and leaving it spick and span.

- Key words: dusting, sweeping, polishing, cobwebs, sparkling and transformed.

Story to tell (in the author's words):
(Based on Acts 2:1-41)

> The 12 apostles (Matthias having replaced Judas) were all together in a house in Jerusalem, when suddenly they became aware of an unusual noise, similar to that of a violent wind blowing. The noise seemed to sweep into the room in which they were sitting, as well as to fill the whole house. And then

what appeared to be tongues of fire followed and came to rest on each of them. As they did so, the apostles were filled with the Holy Spirit. But it wasn't a frightening experience; in fact, there was a feeling of calm and tremendous blessing.

Filled with power from God – the gift that Jesus had promised before his ascension into heaven – the disciples found themselves speaking in different languages. And so, when the 12 went out to talk to the crowd that had gathered in response to hearing the noise, despite the fact that there were people from a number of different countries, everyone was able to hear what the 12 were saying in their own tongue.

'This is amazing: these men are all Galileans, and yet we are able to hear them in our own languages,' was the response of some in the crowd.

But there were also some sceptics. 'Just listen to them. They've had too much to drink.'

After being filled with the power of the Holy Spirit, Peter discovered he possessed a new boldness, and was inspired to preach to the crowd. He spoke about Jesus: his life, death and resurrection – and about Jesus being the way to be set free from sin's consequences and to be filled with eternal promise and hope. Peter implored the crowd to repent and be baptised in the name of Jesus, so that they would be forgiven and receive the gift of the indwelling Holy Spirit. And about 3000 people from that crowd became believers.

Progressively transformed into the likeness of Jesus

The work of the indwelling Holy Spirit is to cleanse and progressively transform our lives – so that we become more like Jesus himself. The Holy Spirit also empowers us to live out the Christian life of love and witness. And he gives us spiritual gifts: special abilities to be used to help build the kingdom, and to bring blessing to others – things like preaching, teaching, prophecy, speaking in other tongues and hospitality.

But the Holy Spirit can only do these things in our lives if we allow him the freedom to do so. And it is a lifelong process. Whatever age we might be, the Holy Spirit hasn't finished with us yet!

Prayer (giving thanks for the indwelling Holy Spirit, and asking for both empowerment and spiritual gifts):

Lord Jesus,
thank you for the gift of the Holy Spirit, which you promised to all believers.
Fill me (us) afresh today, and help me (us) to be willing to allow him complete freedom in my life (our lives) – to cleanse, transform, empower and grant me (us) spiritual gifts to be used to bring blessing to others – an ongoing process.
Help me (us) in my life (our lives) of witness to tell others about you.
And help me (us) to become more like you in the way I (we) live day by day.
I (We) pray that I (we) might see people turning to you in repentance.
Amen.

Finish with the Lord's Prayer.

Harvest

Be still and quiet: Being thankful to God – for the harvest.

Passage to read: Psalm 100.

(Option 1)
To do: Choose a raw ingredient from the larder that comes from a plant. Think about the type of plant it comes from – for example, sugar comes from sugar cane or sugar beet – and then consider the work involved with growing and harvesting it.

(Option 2)
A gentle prompt: A selection of different seeds (and maybe even pots and compost to do some planting).

What do you think? Talk about growing things in the garden.

- Key words: digging, planting, watering, weeding and harvesting.

Story to tell (in the author's words):
(Based on Matthew 13:1-23)

> Jesus told this story:
>   Having prepared the land, a farmer went out to sow some seed. He broadcasted the seed by hand, as usual. And not all of it ended up where it was supposed to go.
>   Some of the seed fell onto the stony path, where it lay in the heat of the day until passing birds swooped down, picked it up and ate it with great relish.

Some of the seed fell onto the rocky ground, where the soil was extremely shallow. The seed grew quickly and looked really good, until the dry weather came . . . And then it was a different story. Blazing sun meant that the shoots withered quickly, both because the plants had no depth of roots and because the shallow soil dried out so quickly.

Some of the seed fell into the undergrowth, among the thorn bushes. Sure enough it grew, but it wasn't long before the thorns choked the young plants.

But the good news is that some of the seed fell onto the good soil that had been carefully prepared; it grew up well and produced a harvest – a really good one at that!

Later on, Jesus explained to his disciples that the parable was all about how people respond to the message about the kingdom.

He compared the birds picking up the seed from the path with the devil snatching away the message from those who hear it but don't understand it.

The seed that fell onto the rocky ground represents those who initially respond excitedly and positively to the message, but it is a shallow response which only lasts until persecution comes.

The seed that fell among the thorns represents those who allow their initial positive response to be overthrown by the busyness and worries of life.

Of course, the seed that fell onto the good soil represents those who hear the message, understand it, make a commitment to following Jesus and ultimately produce spiritual fruit in their lives – a harvest!

Being fruitful

This parable reminds us to give thanks for the harvest: the harvest of the crops, of the sea and of talents – but also the spiritual harvest. It is intended to make us think about our own response to Scripture and our personal journey with Jesus. Where would you place yourself in this? Are you the path, the rocky soil, the thorny ground, or the soil that produces a harvest?

It is never too late in life to produce spiritual fruit (see Galatians 5:22, 23a).

Prayer (being thankful for the physical and spiritual harvest, and seeking to produce spiritual fruit in our own lives):

Creator God,
thank you for your promise that there will be a seedtime and harvest; and for your ongoing provision to me (us), through your creation.
Thank you for the harvest of the crops, sea and talents.
Thank you that there will be a spiritual harvest.
Help me (us) to be truly committed to following Jesus: to understand the message of the kingdom; to withstand persecution; not to allow the busyness or worry of life to swamp my (our) faith; and to constantly produce spiritual fruit in my life (our lives) – whatever stage I (we) might be at in my (our) life's journey.
I (We) remember those who do not have enough to eat or clean water to drink; and place them into your hands.
In Jesus' name.
Amen.

Finish with the Lord's Prayer.

Remembrance

Be still and quiet: Love – loving our neighbour.

Passage to read: Psalm 107:1-9.

(Option 1)
To do: Choose an appropriate item of clothing on which to wear your poppy for Remembrance. Place it in a buttonhole, or carefully pin it securely.

(Option 2)
A gentle prompt: Poppies.

What do you think? Talk about some of the thoughts behind poppies linked with Remembrance: the selfless love of those who gave their lives in battle (bloodshed) to achieve peace for others, and the love of others who grieve for them.

- Key words: battles, medals, sacrifice, peace and selfless love.

Story to tell (in the author's words):
(Based on Luke 10:25-37)

> One of the most well-known parables of Jesus is probably the parable of the Good Samaritan. You may know the story.
>
> A man was travelling from Jerusalem to Jericho. I have always imagined it to be something of a cross-country journey that took the traveller into deserted hilly areas, where bandits could hide out and attack

passing travellers. Sure enough, the man was a victim of robbers: they jumped out and viciously attacked him, took his outer clothing and anything else of any value, and left him seriously injured at the side of the road. His only hope was that someone might come along, take pity on him and offer him help.

The man was convinced that a passing priest would lend a hand – after all, he was a man of God. But the priest passed by without a second glance. I expect he had his reasons why he failed to offer help: maybe he was hurrying to get to an appointment, had other things on his mind or was bound up by religious rules. But there could be no excuse, really!

The next person along the road was a Levite. Surely the Levite would help – or not! He must have been in a hurry as well. Or fearful that the bandits were still lurking, waiting for their next victim to turn up. But some people don't seem to need any excuse not to lend a helping hand or show they care. It can be a sad old world at times, and I'm sure the injured man was beginning to despair of human nature.

The traveller spotted a Samaritan coming towards him. The significance of this was that Jews and Samaritans were not on particularly good terms on the whole. We are led to believe that the injured man, who we assume was a Jew, would not have had high expectations of help from this passer-by. How wrong we can be! Indeed, the Samaritan stopped. He demonstrated great compassion, kindness and generosity as he bandaged the injured man's wounds, lifted him onto his donkey and took him to an inn where he would be safe and cared for – and he even paid for the injured man's stay!

Sharing the love of Jesus

The message is one of loving our neighbour – anyone who is in need. There can be no valid excuse for not exercising Christ-like love in our daily lives. And that love should reach across all barriers of nationality, colour, culture, faith, gender, age, and so on. In his life, and in his death, Jesus is our example of real, unconditional and unselfish love.

During Remembrance we think about, and give thanks for, those who have demonstrated that same kind of selfless love in the fight for peace, as well as those who are still doing so somewhere in the world today – serving in the forces.

We too can live lives demonstrating the same kind of selfless love as Jesus, by being Good Samaritans to those whom we meet day by day – those we know, and those we don't know.

For some in later life, who might be coping with restrictions of movement, travel, memory, the ability to work things out and maybe even communicative skills, the question might arise, 'How can I share the love of Jesus with others?' Love can be demonstrated in so many different ways, including in our response to each other. That could be carers, friends, neighbours or family members – demonstrated even through trying circumstances. A word of thanks or encouragement can be so uplifting. Prayer is a wonderful, loving gift to give to others. And there is nothing quite like a smile that says it all!

Prayer (giving thanks for acts of sacrificial love and remembering those who suffer as a result, and asking for the empowerment to love our neighbours):

Lord Jesus,
thank you for your story about helping our neighbours in times of need.

Fill me (us) with your love for others, and help me (us) to make time to stop and help – even if all I am (we are) able to offer is a kind, helpful or encouraging word, a prayer or a smile.

Thank you for those you place around me (us) who care: carers, family, friends, neighbours, colleagues and even strangers.

Thank you for all those who have selflessly sacrificed their lives for the benefit of others – in the fight for peace and in the service of others.

Be with those who grieve for loved ones lost in these ways, and for those who still suffer from injury of body or mind.

In your name.
Amen.

Finish with the Lord's Prayer.

Christmas

Be still and quiet: Jesus – you can't have Christmas without Christ.

Passage to read: Psalm 13.

(Option 1)
To do: Choose a favourite Christmas carol (using a song book, the internet or from memory). What makes it a favourite?

(Option 2)
A gentle prompt: Nativity set and Christmas cards.

What do you think? Talk about the focus of Christmas cards, which often miss the true meaning of Christmas – the Nativity.

- Key words: greetings, Father Christmas, Christmas trees and the Nativity.

Story to tell (in the author's words):
(Based on Luke 2:8-20)

> Who would have expected it? Would you have expected the first people to be told about the birth of Jesus to have been a group of shepherds out on the hillside? If it had been now, I am sure some local dignitaries would have been invited (a local MP and maybe an influential church leader) – don't you think? But the place of Jesus' birth was also quite

a surprise: the Son of God born in some kind of animal shelter.

Can you imagine the shepherds on the hillside, huddled around a nice warm bonfire, when suddenly the light of the bonfire was swamped by the glory of the Lord shining all around them? I don't know whether that's just like a really bright light? I would imagine it to be something much, much more than that. I use the word 'imagine' quite loosely, because the glory of God is beyond all our imaginations!

First a single angel, then a whole company of angels. And it was to the point: good news, joy, peace and a Saviour born. The angel pointed the shepherds in the right direction to meet with the one person whom the good news was all about: humankind's source of eternal joy and peace – through forgiveness.

After the angels had gone, the shepherds didn't mess about: 'Shall we go and visit, or shall we stay by the fire?' And they didn't get sidetracked about the angelic appearance or even about seeing the glory of God. They hurried off to meet with the baby Jesus for themselves.

After meeting with Jesus, the shepherds went around the neighbourhood telling others about him – and the good news.

Hold on to what really matters at Christmas

Giving presents, eating rich food, bright lights, tinsel, Christmas trees and partying are all associated with Christmas today. Businesses can so often see the 'festive season' as a time to make record profits. For some people it is a time when they end up getting into debt through feeling obliged to spend money they haven't got; and for some it is a time when their loneliness is magnified.

Let's not miss the point this Christmas time: it's actually still about meeting with Jesus, being filled with his peace and joy, receiving forgiveness and knowing eternal hope as a result – and then telling others!

Maybe the festivities of Christmas don't feel as important to you in later life anyway, especially when you are living with health issues. Receive comfort from the true meaning and significance of Christmas.

Prayer (placing Jesus at the centre of Christmas):

Our loving heavenly Father,
thank you for Christmas: the birth of Jesus.
Help me (us) not to allow the bright lights, tinsel and presents to cause me (us) to lose focus on Jesus this Christmas time.
Help me (us) to consider afresh my (our) relationship(s) with him, and increase my (our) faith and commitment.
Let the true meaning of Christmas be proclaimed worldwide this Christmas.
Enable me (us) to feel uplifted by my (our) experience of Jesus at Christmas, even when the festivities might not feel important or be achievable.
In Jesus' name.
Amen.

Finish with the Lord's Prayer.

Men and women of the Old Testament

Adam and Eve

Be still and quiet: Sometimes we make bad choices and disobey God. That has serious consequences, but Jesus can set us free.

Passage to read: Psalm 103:1-6.

(Option 1)
To do: Choose a piece of fruit from the fruit bowl and enjoy eating it.

(Option 2)
A gentle prompt: A bowl of fruit.

What do you think? Talk about your favourite fruit. The story of Adam and Eve doesn't actually say what the forbidden fruit is – though people assume it is an apple.

- Key words: ripe, juicy and good to eat.

Story to tell (in the author's words):
(Based on Genesis 3)

> You probably remember the story of Adam and Eve. It comes right at the beginning of the Bible, straight after the account of God creating the world.
>
> We pick up the story with Adam and Eve settled in the Garden of Eden. Everything was perfect: the garden was a picture of beauty; there were all kinds of amazing animals living in peace and harmony;

God had provided a variety of trees, bushes and plants for food; and there was only one rule to be obeyed: 'Don't eat the fruit from the tree in the middle of the garden . . . Don't even touch it – or you will die,' God warned.

A clear enough warning, you would think! But at the end of the day, God had created Adam and Eve (like us) to have freedom of choice: the opportunity to choose to enter into a close relationship with him from their own free will – or not. Having said that, with freedom of choice can come bad decisions, especially with the devil playing a part in things. Sure enough, the devil turned up in the garden, in the guise of a serpent, and began to spread doubt and lies – as he does.

'Are you sure that's what God said?' he asked. 'Perhaps you misunderstood.'

'I don't think so,' Eve mumbled, as the doubts began to flood into her mind. 'Well, I suppose I could have heard wrongly or misunderstood.'

There was no misunderstanding, but the fruit did look really good to eat: shiny and ripe. Before long, Eve had picked some for herself and given some to Adam – and they were both tucking in to the fruit. Juice was running down their chins. But before they could even say, 'Delicious!' suddenly they realised the seriousness of what they had done. They had disobeyed God, done the one thing he had told them not to do – and after all the amazing love and generosity that he had showered upon them.

When God arrived in the garden later that day, Adam and Eve were hiding because they were so ashamed about what they had done. Their excuse for hiding was that they had no clothes to wear, but that had never bothered them before.

'Have you been eating the fruit from the tree in the middle of the garden?' God asked.

He knew they had!

Adam pointed accusingly at Eve. 'It was her fault!'

Eve blamed the serpent. 'It was his fault!'

But each was responsible for their own actions – as we are, when we deliberately disobey God. And there were consequences: it was the beginning of pain, suffering and death . . . and separation from God.

Set free to enjoy future blessing

Those same consequences apply to us today. But included also in this story is the first prediction of the coming of Jesus – the one who would provide the way for people to be set free from all the consequences of sin. We can be forgiven and restored in our relationship with God, through Jesus – for which we give thanks.

No matter what trials life has placed before us, Genesis 3:15 brings promise of blessing for the eternal future – through the mission of Jesus.

Prayer (giving thanks for forgiveness):

My (Our) loving heavenly Father,
thank you that you love to forgive.
Thank you for Jesus, that through him I (we) can be forgiven.
Forgive me (us) for those bad decisions I (we) have made, which have resulted in me (us) being disobedient to you.
Even when I (we) might be feeling low, help me (us) to

remember your promise of eternal blessing: help me (us) to walk close to Jesus day by day, and to be uplifted by the truth of that promise.

Help our modern Western society not to listen to and be taken in by the devil's deceit and tempting.

In Jesus' name.

Amen.

Finish with the Lord's Prayer.

Noah

Be still and quiet: God never forgets us – he is faithful.

Passage to read: Psalm 29.

(Option 1)
To do: Choose a picture of a favourite pet from the past to look at; grab a cuddly toy to cuddle; or if you still have a pet, spend some time playing with it, cuddling it or just sitting together.

(Option 2)
A gentle prompt: Some photographs of animals (maybe including a favourite pet).

What do you think? Talk about favourite animals. You might like to pick out from the photographs which are farm animals, which are wild animals and which are considered to be pets.

- Key words: cuddly, friendly, bark, purr, bite and scratch.

Story to tell (in the author's words):
(Based on Genesis 6–9)

Imagine how Noah felt when God instructed him to build a boat big enough to house his own family and two of every living creature and bird (male and female) – as well as food. It wasn't as if Noah had any experience of being a boat builder – as far as we know. The big boat was to be called an ark.

The situation was that God was aggrieved about the amount of wickedness that had arisen in the world at that time. Noah and his family were the only people who were still obedient to God, and prepared to listen to him. God's plan was to give creation a fresh start by flooding the earth. The ark would be the only place of safety!

Building such a craft would have been a huge job, much more so than building a rowing boat or a coracle. The ark was to have three decks. Huge amounts of heavy cypress wood would be needed in order to build it, and large quantities of pitch would be required to seal it from the water. And I dare say poor Noah and his family would have had to suffer considerable amounts of scorn and ridicule while pursuing the task.

Some people ask the question: How could the Noah family possibly have rounded up all the different animals to put onto the ark? But the Bible is quite explicit: the animals came on their own, because God sent them!

And so, the boat was completed; Noah, his family, and all the animals were on board, ready for the flood. Imagine how the boat builder must have felt: 'I wonder when it's going to rain.'

And so the waiting began.

But sure enough, the rain came in abundance, and also springs opened up from under the ground. This continued for 40 days and nights. Thankfully, the large vessel rose up in the water and floated majestically over the waves.

Scripture tells us that all through the flood, God never forgot Noah, his family and their precious cargo. Eventually the water subsided, the land dried up and God told Noah that it was safe to disembark.

It was a fresh new start for creation as God led Noah and his party onto the safety of dry land. And God promised that he would never flood the earth in the same way again – and as a sign of his promise he sent the rainbow.

Never forgotten

The Bible is full of amazing promises with eternal potential, including finding a place of safety through a personal relationship with Jesus. The rainbow still reminds us of God's faithfulness in fulfilling his promises. And, of course, when we live in faith and obedience to God, he will never leave or forget us . . . Not even in old age and living with dementia – when it is easy to feel forgotten or left out.

Prayer (thanking God for his faithfulness):

Our loving heavenly Father,
thank you for your faithfulness to me (us): whatever my (our) situation is, and whatever age I (we) might be, you never forget me (us) or abandon me (us).
Thank you for all the wonderful promises in the Bible; and for the sign of the rainbow, which reminds me (us) that you never break your promises.
Reinforce my (our) trust in you.
As I (we) enter into old age and live with dementia, help me (us) not to feel left out or forgotten by people.

I (We) pray that others might turn to you and claim your promises.
In Jesus' name.
Amen.

Finish with the Lord's Prayer.

Joseph

Be still and quiet: We don't always see the bigger picture when we ask, 'Why suffering?'

Passage to read: Psalm 80.

(Option 1)
To do: Choose a favourite piece of clothing from your wardrobe or drawers. What colour is it, and why do you like it so much?

(Option 2)
A gentle prompt: A selection of brightly coloured clothes.

What do you think? Which colours do you like or dislike? Which colours would stand out in public places?

- Key words: bright, striped, patterned, nice, conspicuous and horrible.

Story to tell (in the author's words):
(Based on Genesis 37–50)

We tend to associate Joseph with a brightly coloured coat. The story goes like this:

> Joseph was highly favoured by his father, Jacob. That's why Jacob gave Joseph a brightly coloured coat, when Joseph was 17 years old.
> Today's young people would probably exclaim, 'It's absolutely hideous, Dad! You needn't think I'm going to wear that!'

But for Joseph and his brothers it made the statement, 'This is my favourite son!'

It was unfortunate for the young man because it further damaged what was already a rocky relationship with his older brothers. And to make matters worse, Joseph had two dreams, which he felt appropriate to share with the whole family. The first one involved sheaves of corn in a harvest field; and the second was about the sun, moon and 11 stars. In context, both were suggestive that one day Joseph's parents and brothers would be bowing down to him. Joseph believed this to be a word from God – to be fulfilled in the future. His family believed it to be conceit to the utmost extent. Needless to say, the relationships became even more strained.

From such a privileged position, things very quickly deteriorated. Joseph's brothers were so angry that they sold Joseph into slavery, and then came up with some cock-and-bull story to relay to their poor father. 'Look, Dad, we found his brightly coloured coat – well, at least, we think it was his. He must have been eaten by some ferocious animal. How awful!'

Their father believed what they said and sobbed, 'You're right, my sons: it is his coat – there's no doubt about that. What a terrible thing to happen!'

But while Joseph's dad was mourning his death, the boy was already on his way to Egypt to enter the household of Potiphar.

After a time of prosperity, Joseph ended up in prison following false accusations made against him. It was while he was in there that he discovered a God-given gift of interpreting dreams. In time, this gift enabled Joseph's release from prison in order to interpret Pharaoh's dreams. These dreams were of great significance, as they involved a forthcoming serious famine.

'There will be seven years of plenty, followed by seven years of failed crops,' Joseph explained. 'During the first seven years, food must be put aside for the second seven years. Someone needs to be appointed to organise this.'

Pharaoh selected Joseph as the right man for the job.

And to cut a long story short, years later Joseph's family arrived in Egypt to try and buy food during the famine. They bowed down before Joseph who, by this time, had become very important in those parts. Eventually they were all reunited after Joseph explained who he was, and Pharaoh invited the whole family to come and live in Egypt, where there was still food. Of course, a lot of forgiveness had to take place.

It's not a coincidence

Some might say that Joseph's is a story of coincidences, a lucky outcome. But remember Joseph's dreams in his youth, when God tells him that one day the rest of the family will bow down to him? God allows Joseph to go through times of suffering in order to save his family from inevitable death – and more than that, to enable God's chosen people to survive.

As we get older, we can often look back over our life experiences and realise that in actual fact God's hand has been in those so-called 'coincidences'! (You may wish to talk to a close family member or long-term friend so that you can remember some of these times together.)

Prayer (asking for faith and strength in times of suffering):

Almighty God,
you know the bigger picture, and you know why there are times when I (we) go through difficult experiences and periods of suffering.
You know that, for some, old age is a particular struggle, because of isolation, frailty, disability or sickness.
Be with me (us), especially during such times. Increase my (our) faith and strength to enable me (us) to carry on despite the difficulties, loneliness and suffering.
Be with others who are going through the autumn of life.
Thank you for those glimpses of the bigger picture when I (we) reminisce and realise that those coincidences were your hand at work.
In Jesus' name.
Amen.

Finish with the Lord's Prayer.

Moses

Be still and quiet: God's protection – especially when we feel vulnerable.

Passage to read: Psalm 91:1-8.

(Option 1)
To do: Choose one of the following phrases that best sums up how you are feeling, and complete it:

I feel vulnerable all the time, because . . .

I feel vulnerable some of the time, because . . .

I do not feel vulnerable, because . . .

(Option 2)
A gentle prompt: A Moses basket, some rushes or a photograph of a favourite river.

What do you think? Talk about babies in the family (could be based on memories from the past).

- Key words: changing nappies, feeding, comforting, teething and crying.

Story to tell (in the author's words):
(Based on Exodus 1:1–2:10)

> The story of Moses began in Egypt. The Israelites had moved there to escape a severe famine during the time of Joseph. They had settled down well,

multiplied and become extremely prosperous. Under a new king (or pharaoh), the Egyptians put the Israelites into slavery, treating them ruthlessly and without mercy. The king even gave orders for any male Israelite babies to be killed. But God knew the terrible things that were happening, and in his love and compassion he had a plan to set the Israelites free. The plan began with God choosing Moses to lead the Israelites out of Egypt. But first the baby Moses had to be protected against any harm resulting from the king's orders concerning male Israelite babies.

Moses' parents managed to hide him for three months but, as you can imagine, as the baby grew older, it became more and more difficult to conceal him. Led by God, Moses' mother knew just what to do. She found a basket large enough to place the child in and made it waterproof by coating it with tar and pitch. The idea was to float the child in the little basket, near to where the king's daughter used to bathe each day. Perhaps she would feel sorry for the baby Moses and save him from being killed. Moses' older sister watched as her mother placed the basket among the reeds at the side of the River Nile.

Sure enough, as usual, the beautiful young princess came down to the river's edge to bathe. She was enjoying the water when she heard a baby crying. Following the sound, she eventually found the child. God had his hand on the situation: indeed, it was all part of his bigger plan. The princess felt sorry for Moses and wanted to keep him.

Moses' sister hurried over. 'I know a lady who would look after him for you while he is small.'

The princess was pleased with the suggestion. 'Go and fetch her. I will pay her to nurse him until he gets a little older, and then I will bring him up as my own son.'

So the little girl went to fetch Moses' mother, who was able to take the child home again and care for him until he was old enough to go and live at the palace with the princess.

God's protection

So what can we learn from this story?

In isolation, it is a story about God's protection of Moses during a difficult time. But if we are to include the wider story of Moses, it is about the protection of the Israelites. And its application to us today is that God will protect us – even through the most difficult situations. (For the wider story of Moses, see the book of Exodus.)

There can be feelings of vulnerability in the autumn of life, especially when linked with living with dementia. Things like loss of memory, difficulty working things out, periods of confusion, problems communicating and decreased movement – making independence more of a struggle. At such times we can prayerfully seek God's protection and provision of support.

Prayer (asking that God will protect us when we are feeling vulnerable):

Almighty God,
thank you that you are a powerful God.
Protect me (us), even in the most difficult situations when I am (we are) feeling really vulnerable.

Provide the support I (we) need to help me (us) to maintain
as much independence as possible.
Be with others as they too face difficult or dangerous times.
In Jesus' name.
Amen.

Finish with the Lord's Prayer.

Ruth

Be still and quiet: People who care – depending on others.

Passage to read: Psalm 105:1-22.

(Option 1)
To do: Choose a photograph, an object in the house or even a number on your telephone that reminds you of someone you depend on.

(Option 2)
A gentle prompt: Some photographs of people who care, and a photograph album to put them in.

What do you think? As you work together putting the photographs into the album, talk about who the different people are and how they demonstrate their care. Label the backs of the photographs. You could put them into groups according to the key words.

* Key words: family, friends, neighbours, care worker, etc.

Story to tell (in the author's words):
(Based on Ruth 1–4)

Parts of Ruth's story are extremely sad and traumatic, yet at the same time it is a romantic love story. But the story begins with Naomi.

> As a result of a famine in Judah, Naomi, her husband (Elimelech) and their two sons (Mahlon and

Kilion) went to live in Moab. It wasn't their choice; it was a matter of life or death. The little family were determined to make the best of the situation, but they suffered terrible misfortune. Before long, Elimelech died quite suddenly and unexpectedly. Despite the family's grief, still determined to be positive, the two boys met two local girls – Orpah and Ruth – and got married to them. But still more tragedy hit the family when Mahlon and Kilion died. The only good bit of news that eventually came their way was that, at long last, there was food again in Judah.

Naomi and the two girls prepared to journey back home – well, home for Naomi. Back to Judah.

However, as they set out on the long journey, Naomi turned to Orpah and Ruth and lovingly said, 'Go back to your own homes and families, and I will return to mine. You have been good to me in many ways, but now you must think of your own futures.'

The two daughters-in-law became very emotional as they hugged Naomi. They had become very close to each other during the time they had been together as a family.

'Don't be silly. We won't leave you. We'll come with you to Judah,' they argued.

But the wise old lady wouldn't have it. 'I have nothing to offer you. I don't have any more sons for you to marry. Go home, and you will find someone else with whom you can start a new life.'

Orpah hugged Naomi again. And a tearful 'goodbye' followed as the young lady walked away.

Ruth, on the other hand, was determined that nothing would separate her from her friend and mother-in -law.

'Please don't send me away. I want to come with you wherever you go. I want your God to be my God. I want your people to be my people. My desire is that only death will eventually part us,' Ruth declared.

Naomi was surprised. Ruth probably surprised herself a little, with such a declaration of total commitment. What could Naomi say in reply? And so the two women returned to Bethlehem in Judah to pick up the pieces. Well . . . so they thought. In actual fact, it was more like a fresh new start.

While working hard to provide food for herself and Naomi, Ruth fell in love with a young farmer called Boaz. One of the conditions of the young couple being able to get married was that Boaz had to buy the land that had belonged to Elimelech, to keep it in the family. Of course, he was more than happy to do that. So Boaz and Ruth got married and then had a son called Obed (who became grandfather to King David). What a wonderful ending to the story!

Learning to depend on others

Ruth's story is crucial to the ancestry into which Jesus is born. It is a story about redemption: just as Boaz enables Ruth to be free to marry him, through paying the price for Elimelech's land, Jesus has paid the penalty for our sin, so that we might be free to enter into an eternal and personal relationship with him (and experience his forgiveness through that relationship). And it is a story about commitment and hope, and illustrates that we sometimes need to learn to depend on others in difficult times – for example, times of sickness, frailty or old age.

Prayer (to learn to depend on others – especially God):

Almighty God,

thank you that I (we) can depend on you, and that in times of need you also place others around me (us) on whom I (we) can depend. But it can sometimes be difficult to overcome my (our) feelings of independence. Help me (us) to do that.

Thank you that through Jesus paying the penalty for sin, he has made it possible for all of humankind to enter into an eternal, personal relationship with him – and thus with you and the Holy Spirit – and to be forgiven.

Help me (us) to repentantly and in faith depend on Jesus as my (our) Lord and Saviour.

Be with all those who have had to learn to depend on others, in different ways and for different reasons.

In Jesus' name.

Amen.

Finish with the Lord's Prayer.

David

Be still and quiet: Defeating those things that seem very big and frightening in our lives, with God's help; finding the enablement to live our lives when facing those things.

Passage to read: Psalm 1.

(Option 1)
To do: Choose a photograph which brings back memories. Hopefully some of those memories are of happy times, but they might also be tinged with sad or difficult associations. Spend some time remembering.

(Option 2)
A gentle prompt: Some items symbolic of things like old age, sickness, disability, loneliness, sadness, etc. (i.e. those things that may seem very big and frightening) – things such as a walking stick, a medicine spoon or a disability badge.

What do you think? Talk about these and other life experiences that you might be struggling to cope with.

- Key words: big, frightening, lonely, challenging and limiting.

Story to tell (in the author's words):
(Based on 1 Samuel 17)

> David was one of those people who went through childhood appearing to be no one special – and I don't mean that in a contemptuous way. He was

a shepherd boy, which would have been looked upon as a very ordinary job at the time. I suppose the first real surprise came when Samuel visited and announced that God had chosen the young shepherd boy to be the next king . . . but in the meantime, life just carried on as normal.

David's first real break was when he was summoned to King Saul because of his ability to play the harp. His attendants thought it might help when the king was in a bad humour. Saul took to the young man, requesting that he should become part of the staff in the royal palace. And so, after that, David would spend some of his time with King Saul and some back at home caring for his father's sheep.

All was well until the Philistines turned up – with no good intentions towards the Israelites. There was one particular warrior in their midst, who was called Goliath. He was really tall and strong, and quite 'in your face'.

'Come and fight me,' he challenged. 'Nominate someone, and if they kill me, the Philistines will be your subjects. And if not,' he grinned, 'you will become our subjects.'

Goliath had that intimidating manner. Everyone was afraid of this huge man. He made his challenge twice a day for 40 days, and nobody was brave enough to face him.

About this time it happened that his father, Jesse, asked David to go and visit his brothers who were in Saul's army, to take them a food hamper, and then to report back how they were. Not by chance, I am sure! To everyone's surprise, young David volunteered to go and fight Goliath. I expect there was some laughter and scornful remarks made before David was taken seriously. Saul tried to get David to wear a fine suit of armour, but it was not what the brave young shepherd boy was used to. All he needed was his sling, a few small pebbles and God with him.

Goliath was filled with anger, insulted that the Israelites would send a shepherd boy out to fight him. He used some choice words as he literally looked down on David.

But David refused to be intimidated as he confidently replied, 'God is on my side.'

The battle was soon over, as the mighty Philistine warrior fell to the floor after one of the pebbles dealt him a fatal blow. The young man David knew that the victory belonged to God.

David went on to be a great king. The battle with Goliath was just the beginning of his life of trust in God. If we were to look at the wider story of David we would discover that he had to face many big and frightening situations during his rule as king. (For the wider story of David, see 1 Samuel 16–31; the book of 2 Samuel; and 1 Kings 1:1–2:12.)

Coping with those things in our lives that appear to be 'big and frightening'

God will help us to deal with the things that seem very big and frightening in our lives: those difficult decisions we have to make; times of acute sadness or regret; periods of sickness or suffering in our lives or the lives of those we are close to; getting old; failing health; not coping; fears and anxieties . . . Whatever those big and frightening things might be in our lives, when we include God and ask for his help and sustenance, he will either overcome them or give us the strength to carry on despite our circumstances. Either way, we share in his victory!

Prayer (for help to face the things that seem very big and frightening in our lives):

Mighty God,

thank you that I am (we are) not on my (our) own as I (we) face those things that seem very big and frightening in my life (our lives).

You know the things that I am (we are) struggling with at the moment: maybe difficult decisions I (we) have to make; times of acute sadness or regret; periods of sickness or suffering in my life (our lives) or the lives of those I am (we are) close to; those fears; and all the anxieties.

(You may add your own specific situation(s) and struggle(s) you battle with – and/or those of others.)

Strengthen and sustain me (us): help me (us) either to overcome those things that seem very big and frightening in my life (our lives); or, at least, enable me (us) to carry on despite my (our) circumstances.

In Jesus' name.

Amen.

Finish with the Lord's Prayer.

Jonah

Be still and quiet: God is everywhere – we can't run away from him!

Passage to read: Psalm 91:9-16.

(Option 1)
To do: Choose a favourite part of the world (using a globe, an atlas or the internet). It might be a location where you have lived, worked or holidayed. Remember that wherever it might be, God is there!

(Option 2)
A gentle prompt: A globe or world map.

What do you think? Talk about God being everywhere, even in the most desolate desert or the darkest jungle. You might also like to point to some of the places in the world that you have visited.

- Key words: flight, cruise, drive, abroad, United Kingdom and journey.

Story to tell (in the author's words):
(Based on Jonah 1–4)

I wonder if you have ever tried to run away from anyone.

Having been called by God to go and preach against the wickedness in Nineveh – a job that didn't really appeal very much – Jonah thought he could outrun God. He hastened down to Joppa.

'Can you take me to Tarshish?' he pleaded as he scrambled on board a boat that was moored in the docks.

The old sea captain nodded. 'It'll cost you.'

Jonah paid his fare and then found somewhere comfortable to lie down and have a sleep. He was convinced that before long he would be out of reach of God. How wrong you can be!

It wasn't very long at all before the wind got up, the waves got bigger, and the little boat began to be tossed precariously in the rough sea – so much so that everyone feared for their lives. Well, everyone except Jonah, because he was still fast asleep.

'Get up and start praying harder than you've ever done before,' the captain commanded as he poked the sleeping man.

Jonah woke up with a start. 'What's all the fuss about?'

Suddenly the boat rolled precariously, throwing the two men across the floor. 'That's what the fuss is all about!'

It was decided to cast lots to see whose fault this horrendous storm could be. Of course, Jonah drew the short straw. 'What have you been up to, that has made your God so angry?'

At long last, Jonah realised that it was impossible to run away from God, so he gave the sailors the instruction, 'Throw me overboard and save yourselves.'

He probably didn't expect to be taken up on that – in fact, he wasn't to start with – but then out of desperation the crew picked up poor Jonah and tossed him into the raging sea.

The sea grew calm. Jonah didn't have to swim too far, because God sent a huge fish to swallow him – and keep him safe. It smelled a bit inside the fish and wasn't particularly comfortable, but it gave Jonah time to really focus on God – and to do some more praying. In fact, he did lots of praying!

Three long days and three long nights later, the big fish vomited Jonah out onto the beach; and once again came the call of God: 'Go to Nineveh.'

This time Jonah obeyed, and passed on God's message: 'God's not at all happy with you lot; you've been very wicked.'

To Jonah's surprise, everyone repented, and God forgave them. And the story finished with Jonah not really understanding the depth of God's love, compassion and forgiveness – until God gave him a little visual demonstration.

We can't run away from God

The story of Jonah is about a God of love, compassion and forgiveness; but it is also about a God we can't run away from, however much we might try. Because God is everywhere!

Some people spend their whole lives trying to run away from God.

Prayer (thanking God for his love, compassion and forgiveness, and the fact that he is everywhere):

Heavenly Father,
thank you that wherever I am (we are), I am (we are) always in your presence – I (we) can never run away from you.

Thank you for your love, compassion and forgiveness.

Help me (us), like the people from Nineveh, to turn to you in repentance and trust – if I (we) haven't already.

If I am (we are) trying to run away from you, like Jonah at the beginning of the story, help me (us) to stop running – and to be obedient to your calling and will.

And I (we) pray for others who might be running away from you at this time.

In Jesus' name.

Amen.

Finish with the Lord's Prayer.

People who meet with Jesus

The tempter

Be still and quiet: Trusting in the truth of the Bible – God's word.

Passage to read: Psalm 33:1-11.

(Option 1)
To do: Choose a favourite Bible passage. Why is it such a favourite? Maybe it brings back memories of a special time in your life. Perhaps it has been a great comfort or help to you on a variety of occasions. It might offer great comfort and hope to you at the present time.

(Option 2)
A gentle prompt: A selection of books, including the Bible – some factual and some fiction.

What do you think? Talk about fact and fiction: truth and lies.

- Key words: doubt, deceive, untrue, half true and not real.

Story to tell (in the author's words):
(Based on Matthew 4:1-11)

> After Jesus' baptism, the Holy Spirit led him into the desert to have some quiet time with God, to prepare for his forthcoming ministry. For 40 days and nights Jesus fasted, as he spent time in prayer and thought, listening to what the Father was saying to him. We can imagine Jesus being really hungry by the end of

this time, and that's when the tempter popped in to try to lead Jesus away from the plans and purposes of God – because that is what he does!

'I expect you're feeling peckish now,' the tempter observed. 'Easily solved, though. You could turn those stones into bread – and have a real feast.'

But Jesus wasn't to be taken in: he pointed the devil to the Scriptures where it says quite emphatically that we need more than physical food to satisfy – we need the word of God (the Bible).

The tempter took Jesus to Jerusalem, to the highest point of the temple. 'Talking of the Scriptures, it says that the angels will protect you. Prove to me that you really are the Son of God by jumping off here, and we'll see who comes to save you.'

Jesus pointed the devil to another part of the Scriptures where it tells us not to put God to the test.

'Okay!' the tempter announced as he took Jesus to a very high mountain and pointed to all the cities, towns and villages scattered around. 'Look! If you would bow down and worship me – do things my way – then all this could be yours.'

Once again Jesus pointed the devil to the Scriptures where it tells us to worship and serve God – and no one else. Jesus commanded the devil to go. With that, the devil left and angels came to minister to Jesus.

Find strength and guidance from God's word

This is a warning to us. The tempter is never far away, and he will always tempt us when we are at our weakest: hungry, thirsty, lonely, stressed, tired, anxious, discouraged, upset . . .

But it's not wrong to be tempted: it only becomes sin if we give in to that temptation. Remember, Jesus is our guide and example: we too must look to the truth of the Bible when we face temptation.

Some people collect stamps; others collect teapots . . . and still others accumulate verses of Scripture in their memories during the course of their life's journey – that is such a valuable resource to have!

Prayer (giving thanks for the truth and guidance of the Bible, and asking for understanding):

My (Our) loving heavenly Father,

thank you for the truth of the Bible: as well as being full of wonderful promises and guidance, it has the answers for when I am (we are) faced with difficult decisions and find myself (ourselves) in situations of temptation.

Thank you for those precious and useful verses that I (we) have been able to recall or turn to at different times in my life (our lives).

Help me (us) through the power of the Holy Spirit to read and understand more of the Bible, and to put into practice those things that I (we) learn.

Strengthen me (us) as I (we) face temptation – help me (us) to say 'No!'

Be with and speak to those who are struggling to find answers at this time.

In Jesus' name.

Amen.

Finish with the Lord's Prayer.

Some fishermen

Be still and quiet: Fishing for people – witnessing to and sharing our own story with others; what Jesus has done for me!

Passage to read: Psalm 30.

(Option 1)
To do: Choose a favourite story, parable or verse from the Bible that has always encouraged you in your faith.

(Option 2)
A gentle prompt: Fishing rods, nets, bait, etc.

What do you think? Share any fishing stories: the one that got away!

- Key words: rod, hook, bait, net and catch.

Story to tell (in the author's words):
(Based on Matthew 4:18-22)

> I guess it would not have been an unfamiliar sight while walking beside the Sea of Galilee to see fishermen making repairs on their boats, preparing their nets and setting out to fish. But it was no accident or coincidence that Jesus had set out to walk along that path on this particular day. He had started out on a mission, with the aim of finding four particular fishermen to ask them a very special question.

We can imagine the scene: a bright, warm, sunshiny day. The fishermen were busy preparing to go out fishing, unaware of passers-by. Jesus was walking along, enjoying the views across the water, feeling the sun on his face, watching all the different fishermen about their business, and listening to the hungry birds always looking for scraps of fish. Perhaps there was a fishiness about the air. But remember, Jesus was on a mission to look for four particular fishermen.

At last he spotted the first two: Simon Peter and his brother Andrew. They were already out on the lake casting their net with the skill and expertise of true fishermen. Jesus watched for a few moments before shouting across the water to them.

'Will you follow me, and then I will teach you how to fish people into the kingdom?'

Maybe Simon Peter and Andrew had met with Jesus before, but it was still a big ask: after all, he was asking them to give up their business – their livelihood. They could have been forgiven for requesting time to think about it – or at least, to make arrangements. But there was none of that: in came the net, they sailed the little boat back to the shore and followed Jesus without a second thought.

A little further along the shore, Jesus saw James and his brother John in their boat getting their net ready, with their father Zebedee. Jesus called the two boys, and immediately they walked away from the family business to follow him.

Following Jesus and then sharing our story with others

That's quite something: to leave everything and immediately follow Jesus. It's about relationship and priority. Jesus wants to be in a personal relationship with each one of us today, and he wants us to make it a priority to follow him. Following Jesus means following his teaching and guidance, striving to be more like him and having a close relationship with him – walking with him day by day.

Maybe Jesus has been the main priority in your life for many years now – or maybe not.

I think our priorities often change as we get older: material objects that may have seemed so important in the past suddenly don't seem as important any more. Perhaps now is the time to consider entering into that relationship with Jesus – if you haven't done so already.

However, the essence of this story is really about telling other people the good news: of forgiveness, a second chance and eternal hope available through Jesus. When we have entered into a personal relationship with Jesus ourselves, we should talk to others about our experience, as well as about what the Bible teaches, to help lead them closer to Jesus (part of the process of fishing people into the kingdom). And there's a lot of fishing still to be done in the world around us: people who need to hear about Jesus. Those people are often closer to home than we might imagine, and it is something we can all do.

Prayer (having the courage to speak to others about Jesus):

Lord Jesus,
thank you for your offer of forgiveness, a second chance and eternal hope through a relationship with you.

Help me (us) to walk closer to you each day of my life (our lives): to know you better, to trust you more, to listen to your guidance and to strive to become increasingly like you.

Give me (us) the courage and the right words to say when I (we) have the opportunity to speak to others about you, and my (our) relationship with you.

Make me a fisher (us fishers) of men.

Fill me (us) afresh with the power of your Holy Spirit to do that.

Prepare the hearts and minds of those to whom I (we) will speak about you.

In your name.

Amen.

Finish with the Lord's Prayer.

Matthew

Be still and quiet: Called to follow Jesus – making an immediate response.

Passage to read: Psalm 42.

(Option 1)
To do: Choose from the following list the qualities you associate with living a Christ-like lifestyle, and those you don't: love, generosity, lies, greed, aggression, forgiveness, immorality and hope.

(Option 2)
A gentle prompt: Wedding invitation, party invitation, etc.

What do you think? Talk about being invited to special occasions and events, and the instruction RSVP. It is easy to miss the deadline!

- Key words: weddings, parties, presentations and celebrations.

Story to tell (in the author's words):
(Based on Matthew 9:9-13)

> It was just another day for Matthew as he sat at his tax-collecting booth, collecting taxes. In reality, it probably hadn't been his first choice of job, although it did pay quite well. But being renowned for dishonesty and working on behalf of the Romans didn't make the tax collectors of the time very popular with the Jews.

We can imagine Matthew dealing with a queue of disillusioned people on this occasion, who were angry at being exploited once again. Already his day had probably been coloured by resentment from his customers. But then he looked up to see Jesus' loving face smiling at him.

'Good afternoon, Matthew.' Enough to brighten anyone's day. 'I've come to invite you to follow me.'

I would have expected a few questions to be asked. But no: Matthew jumped up excitedly and with determination. He pulled the shutters down, banged the door behind him and hurried over to where Jesus was standing.

'Here I am! Let's go then!'

Later that day, Matthew threw a dinner party. All sorts of people were there, including tax collector friends and some other people who did not win the approval of the local community.

The Pharisees were never far away from Jesus, and on this particular evening they approached some of his disciples – to criticise. 'What's going on here: tax collectors, people of dubious character, and Jesus in their midst? Why? Why can't your teacher find some better friends to mix with?'

Jesus overheard their scathing comments. 'People who are ill need to see the doctor; wouldn't you agree?' They nodded. 'Well, my ministry is to those who are spiritually sick. I can reach and help those who know they have disobeyed God; but not those who like to think they're perfect.'

The Pharisees probably missed the point on that occasion.

Making a response to Jesus

What Jesus is saying is that we have all done things wrong, fallen short of God's standards – and that's what his mission is all about. But in order to receive Jesus' forgiveness, a fresh start and hope for eternity, we need to follow him in the knowledge and acceptance that we have all sinned. Those who think that they are living perfect lives are deluded, and are not in a position of being able to benefit from the salvation Jesus offers.

In the story, Matthew responds immediately and decisively to Jesus' invitation to follow him. What is your response? Remember there is no age limit!

Prayer (that we might make a positive response to Jesus):

Dear Lord Jesus,
thank you that your mission is to sinners – that's everyone!
Thank you for the opportunity to follow you: to be forgiven, to be given a second chance and to be filled with eternal hope.
Help me (us) to respond positively to your invitation to follow you, and not to put off that decision.
Help me (us) to walk closer to you each day.
I (We) pray for those who still refuse to turn to you.
In your name.
Amen.

Finish with the Lord's Prayer.

Mary and Martha

Be still and quiet: Being still – and listening to Jesus.

Passage to read: Psalm 46.

(Option 1)
To do: Choose a place in the house or garden where you can sit quietly with Jesus, for 10 or 15 minutes. Listen to what he has to say to you – it might be, 'Rest in my presence.'

(Option 2)
A gentle prompt: A selection of cookery books.

What do you think? Talk about your favourite food – either to cook or to eat. Would you give it to guests?

- Key words: savoury, pudding, cake, sweets and chocolates.

Story to tell (in the author's words):
(Based on Luke 10:38-42)

> Martha had always been a busy sort of person. She couldn't bear to see a job that needed doing around the house and not attend to it. And when she had people round to entertain, she just wanted everything to be perfect for them – well, as near to perfect as anyone could manage. The house had to be spotless, warm, comfortable and inviting. The food had to be fresh, tasty and plentiful. And nothing would ever be too much trouble.

On this particular occasion Martha had invited Jesus and his disciples to come round. Despite all the preparations beforehand, as soon as they arrived she began to bustle around, making sure that everything was okay for her guests. It wasn't that she wanted to show off, or that she was obsessive about household chores; she just wanted it to be nice and welcoming.

As Martha hurried around, she became irritated by her sister Mary who could have been helping but had chosen to sit near Jesus' feet, listening to his wonderful stories about the kingdom. Martha thought to herself, 'Doesn't she think I would like to have sat down in Jesus' company for a few minutes as well? But someone has to do the work.' In the end, Martha could stand it no longer: fuming, she hurried over to Jesus.

'Will you tell my sister to come and help me, please – she has left me to do everything. Now I am worn out.'

I am sure Jesus will have smiled warmly and answered with compassion and not as a reprimand for his dear friend. 'Martha, it is not good for you to put yourself under so much stress, worrying about unnecessary things. Mary has made the better choice; one which I cannot go against.'

Being still and quiet in Jesus' presence

I am sure we have sympathy for Martha and her good intentions; maybe we associate with her busyness in our own lives. We live in a very busy world, where even leisure time at home seems to be filled with phone calls, emails, the internet, radio, TV . . . maybe even carers, family members, friends or neighbours dropping in. Many of those are things that have some good and positive benefits, but where in the midst of all the noise and busyness do we find time for God? Time when we are still and quiet with Jesus, to listen to what he has to say to us and to rest in his presence?

Martha is filled with good intentions, but good intentions are not enough: we need to do the right thing. Mary has made the better choice – to be still and quiet as she learns from Jesus!

Even in the autumn of life it can be difficult to find the time to be still and quiet in Jesus' presence (especially in residential care or with carers coming in regularly) – but it is still important.

Prayer (seeking the time to be still and quiet in the presence of Jesus):

Loving Lord Jesus,
thank you that you want to spend time with me (us).
Help me (us) to make the time to put aside the busyness of the day to be still and quiet in your presence.
Help me to be a good listener (us to be good listeners) to what you have to say to me (us), and to respond positively.
Help me (us) to allow myself (ourselves) to rest in your presence, and to be spiritually refreshed – especially if my body is (our bodies are) beginning to feel frail and tired, or my memory (our memories) are not as good as it (they) used to be.
Also, encourage other people to rest in your presence and experience that same kind of refreshment.
Amen.

Finish with the Lord's Prayer.

Zacchaeus

Be still and quiet: Loved, accepted and transformed – all through meeting with Jesus.

Passage to read: Psalm 138.

(Option 1)
To do: Choose from the following feelings; decide which is the most important to you at this time: to be loved, accepted, valued, encouraged or respected.

(Option 2)
A gentle prompt: Photographs or memorabilia of famous people.

What do you think? Talk about people you have met, and the impact they have had on you.

- Key words: example, inspirational, uplifting and unforgettable.

Story to tell (in the author's words):
(Based on Luke 19:1-10)

> Zacchaeus was a chief tax collector, and he was wealthy. That, together with the fact that he worked for the Romans and was probably ripping off his fellow countrymen, made him rather unpopular. As for his riches – material wealth has the habit of only satisfying for a limited time. The proof of the

pudding was quite simply that, all in all, Zacchaeus was quite a sad person. Indeed, he really appeared to be searching for some kind of meaning and purpose to his life. And, I guess, for someone to love and accept him. It was in the course of this search that Zacchaeus wanted to see Jesus when he passed through Jericho. He had no aspirations to meet him – to see him would be sufficient.

Zacchaeus was far from tall, and no one was going to do him any favours like making room for him at the front of the crowd. He decided to climb a tree, so that he could see above people's heads.

The excitement and related level of noise increased considerably as Jesus was spotted in the distance.

'Get ready, he's on his way!'

Zacchaeus leaned forwards very carefully, for fear of losing his balance. He was reluctant to cheer too loudly, just in case he drew attention to himself. So he contented himself by having a fidget around to make himself comfortable, in preparation for the important moment. Remember that Zacchaeus just wanted to see Jesus – nothing more.

Zacchaeus could hardly contain his excitement as Jesus came ever closer. His gaze moved away from the large crowd below his perch – the same crowd to which he desired to be inconspicuous – and centred solely on Jesus. I repeat that Zacchaeus had no expectation for anything more than just to see Jesus.

Moments later, Jesus stopped under the tree – the same tree that Zacchaeus was sitting in. He looked up. 'Zacchaeus, come down. I was hoping to come to your house for some refreshments and a chat.'

Words probably failed Zacchaeus. He had only ever thought he would see Jesus, but now he was to meet him personally. This could change his whole life. There were murmurs among the crowd.

'Fancy taking notice of someone like him!'

'Who'd have thought Jesus would choose to be the guest of a sinner?!'

'It's not fair!'

But Zacchaeus already felt loved and accepted by Jesus.

The crowd waited in anticipation: Would this be 'payback' time for this sinner who had swindled them time and time again? They didn't have to wait too long to find out. It was a transformed Zacchaeus who hurried out with Jesus, carrying a large bag of money.

'I'm going to pay back all those people I have cheated – fourfold. And I am going to give half my money to the poor.'

The crowd were taken aback – speechless!

Jesus looked on with satisfaction: after all, his mission was – and still is – to seek and to save the lost.

The power of love and acceptance

Meeting with Jesus and entering into a personal relationship with him is life changing, with a significance that goes on forever – even after death. It's not just about feeling loved and accepted by him. Through that relationship, we are forgiven for all the things we have done wrong, and we are transformed by the indwelling Holy Spirit. And the evidence of such a relationship will be there for others to see and experience.

As age creeps steadily on and youth gets left behind –
especially when it brings with it something like dementia – it
is easy to feel that society no longer accepts us in the same
way – but Jesus loves and accepts us just as we are!

Prayer (giving thanks that we are loved and accepted by Jesus):

Lord Jesus,

thank you that you love and accept me (us) just as I am (we are).
Thank you that through meeting with you and entering into
a personal relationship with you, I am (we are) forgiven and
transformed – and my life is (our lives are) made complete.

Thank you that your mission is to seek and to save the lost.

Help me (us) to strive for an ever closer relationship with
you, and to experience the transforming power of the Holy
Spirit fully in my life (our lives).

Let the evidence of my (our) relationship with you be
unmistakably present in my life (our lives) for others to
experience.

I (We) pray for all those who are still seeking, in the same way
that Zacchaeus is at the beginning of his story.

In your name.

Amen.

Finish with the Lord's Prayer.

Nicodemus

Be still and quiet: Physical death – and eternal life.

Passage to read: Psalm 39 (note in particular verse 7b).

(Option 1)
To do: Choose some different coloured felt tip pens, coloured pencils, pastels or paints; and on a sheet of paper sketch or paint a picture of what you believe heaven will be like.

(Option 2)
A gentle prompt: A fairly easy jigsaw puzzle to make up together.

What do you think? Talk about seeing the bigger picture: i.e. the difference between looking at one or two pieces of jigsaw joined together and seeing the completed puzzle. Compare it with God seeing the eternal picture.

- Key words: death, resurrection and eternal life.

Story to tell (in the author's words):
(Based on John 3:1-21)

> Why might someone deliberately decide to go out visiting at night when it's dark? Perhaps because they don't want to be seen by anyone!
>
> Nicodemus was a Pharisee and a member of the Jewish ruling council. You could say that he was quite an important and influential person – and

he did not want to be seen mixing with the likes of Jesus and his disciples for fear of repercussions. So he went to visit Jesus at night, to ask him some questions about things that had been puzzling him.

'To perform the amazing miracles that I've observed, you must be from God,' he began.

Jesus sensed that Nicodemus was curious about the kingdom of God and wanted to clarify the situation. 'There is only one way to enter into the kingdom, and that is by being born again.'

Nicodemus looked confused. 'How can someone be born a second time? It is not possible to enter into a mother's womb again.'

Jesus repeated, 'There is only one way to enter into the kingdom, and that is by being born again.' He clarified: 'Of the Spirit.'

Nicodemus still didn't understand. 'How can this happen?'

Jesus went on to predict his death on the cross, and to explain that as a result people would enter into God's eternal kingdom through believing in him. He emphasised how much God loved the world in order to do that: so that people could be saved from the consequences of sin.

Interestingly, later on Nicodemus accompanied Joseph of Arimathea to bury Jesus' body in the tomb – after his crucifixion. It would certainly appear that he had made a positive response to Jesus and his teaching.

Entering into a new life that is eternal

In a world where physical death is expected – and feared by many – Jesus offers the opportunity to enter into his eternal kingdom, and to live forever in his presence. The way into that kingdom is to place our belief in Jesus, to symbolically die to our old sinful lifestyle and to be reborn into a new lifestyle, living according to Jesus' teaching and example. We cannot be reborn in a physical sense, but we can be reborn spiritually! And it is possible to be reborn at any age!

Prayer (recognising and responding to the opportunity to be reborn into a new way of life):

Our loving heavenly Father,
thank you that you love me (us) so much that you allowed Jesus to die on the cross, paying the penalty for my (our) sin – and he rose again.
Thank you that as a result I (we) can be reborn spiritually and enter into the kingdom for ever.
Help me (us) to place my (our) belief in Jesus, to symbolically die to my (our) old sinful way(s) of life and to be reborn into a new way of life based on following Jesus' teaching and example.
Enable those who are searching to understand what it means to be reborn spiritually – and that it can happen at any age.
In Jesus' name.
Amen.

Finish with the Lord's Prayer.

The woman at the well

Be still and quiet: Hope.

Passage to read: Psalm 25.

(Option 1)
To do: Choose something nice to eat or drink, but only a very small portion. Feel what it is like to eat but not have your hunger satisfied, or to drink and not have your thirst quenched.

(Option 2)
A gentle prompt: A jug of water and some glasses.

What do you think? Talk about having a drink, and then being thirsty again.

- Key words: parched, dehydrated, iced water, slice of lemon and refreshed.

Story to tell (in the author's words):
(Based on John 4:1-26, 39-42)

> Jesus arrived at Jacob's well in Samaria. He was hot and tired, so he found somewhere comfortable to sit. Soon a woman from that area approached to draw some water.
>
> 'Would you give a drink to a weary traveller?' Jesus asked.
>
> The woman was aware that Jews and Samaritans didn't usually associate with each other, and asked,

'Are you sure you want me to get you a drink?'

'If you knew who I am,' Jesus replied, 'you would be asking me for the gift of living water.'

The woman was confused and argued, 'But you don't have a bucket to draw water from the well. Where are you going to get this living water from? Are you more powerful than Jacob who provided this well?'

Jesus smiled. 'If you drink of this living water, you will never be thirsty again. In fact, it will bring you eternal life.'

The woman said, 'All right, then; let me have some. Then I will never have to come to collect water from this well again.'

Jesus encouraged the woman, 'Go and fetch your husband to share in this conversation.'

'I don't have a husband,' came the reply.

'You have answered truthfully,' Jesus told her. 'The man you are living with is not your husband, though you have had five husbands in the past.'

The woman was amazed. 'You must be some kind of prophet to know that!' Then, trying to change the subject, she commented, 'There has been some dispute about where is the right place to worship.'

Jesus explained, 'The place of worship is not the real issue. The real issue is how you worship – remember salvation is coming through Jewish lines.'

'I've heard about the Messiah coming,' the woman replied.

There was a moment of silence before Jesus stated, 'I am the Messiah.'

Through the woman telling her friends and neighbours about meeting with Jesus, many Samaritans came to him and begged him to stay. As a result of Jesus staying on for another two days, and through his ministry, many believed that he really was the Saviour of the world, and they put their trust in him.

Discovering hope

This is a story primarily about being able to possess eternal hope. Jesus is still the one who offers salvation to us today. If we believe that he is the Messiah – the one who came to set humankind free from the consequences of sin – and we accept him as our Lord and Saviour, then we will receive that hope which nothing can take away. At times in the autumn of life we may reach the point of feeling that almost all we have left is that hope.

Prayer (giving thanks for and claiming the hope that is available through Jesus):

My (Our) Lord and Saviour Jesus Christ,
thank you that you are the one who came to earth to bring salvation to humankind.
Thank you that you have brought hope to a world that would otherwise be hopeless.
Help me (us) to believe and trust in you.
Forgive me (us) for the things I (we) have done wrong in my life (our lives), and help me (us) to accept you as my (our) Lord and Saviour.
Fill me (us) with eternal hope, particularly as I (we) face old age and maybe failing health, when everything seems to be a struggle.

I (We) pray that you will lead all those who are feeling hopeless to discover hope through a relationship with you.
In your name.
Amen.

Finish with the Lord's Prayer.

PART FOUR

Additional resources

Prayers in response to how I'm feeling

If necessary, ask a friend, family member or carer to say each phrase first for you to repeat.

Feeling frightened (the effects of old age)

Almighty God,
thank you that you are a powerful God and the God of miracles.
Right now, I need to feel your strong arms around me:
    protecting me in this time of fear;
    guiding me when everything seems uncertain;
    holding me up, when I feel that my world is dropping away from underneath me;
    being strong in my weakness.
I am fearful of what is happening as I become wearier, less mobile, forget things and am generally feeling the effects of a body that is getting old.
I am fearful of what the future holds, whether I will be able to cope and keep some independence.
Please be with me at all times:
    surround me with your love;
    grant me peace;
    and fill me with eternal hope through my relationship with Jesus.
In his name.
Amen.

Feeling frightened (having been diagnosed with dementia)

Loving heavenly Father,
thank you that you are a powerful God.
    I need to experience your power in my life right now.
    I need to be able to overcome the fears.
    I need the strength and courage to move forwards in my life.
    I need the encouragement to carry on living life to the full.
I am feeling so fearful because I have been diagnosed with dementia:
    fearful of what I know about the condition;
    fearful of what I don't know about how it will affect me;
    fearful of what I can't remember;
    and too fearful to make any plans.
Please stay with me during the good times and the difficult ones, and never stop loving or caring for me.
Uphold my family and friends during the time ahead.
And place people around me who have positive caring attitudes; who will help me to still experience joy and fulfilment in my life.
In Jesus' name.
Amen.

Feeling frightened (not being able to cope)

Gracious God,
thank you that you understand how I feel, and why I feel like it – and that you care.
    It's one of my greatest fears.
    I don't feel that I am coping any more.
    Chores around my home and garden are being neglected.
Please help me to discover new ways to carry out some of the more basic tasks.

Point me towards various aids and technology to help me to perform some of the more difficult tasks.
Place around me people who are willing to take over those important tasks that I really can't do myself.
And take away the worry of those tasks that aren't going to get done at all.
In Jesus' name.
Amen.

Feeling frightened (of death)

Lord Jesus,
I need assurance concerning my eternal future:
    to know that death is not the end;
    to be reassured of my salvation through you;
    and to overcome the fear of dying.
Thank you for your words in John 14, which say that:
    your followers don't need to be worried or anxious;
    you are preparing a place for us;
    and you will come to take us to be with you there.
Please help me to believe the promises in the Bible, and to find comfort and hope through them – and in my relationship with you.
Amen.

Feeling lonely

Loving heavenly Father,
thank you that you are always with me. It is a great comfort, but I still feel lonely.
Loneliness isn't about me not realising that you are with me; it's not even just about whether or not friends, family or carers are in my home.

Loneliness can sometimes be about not being able to get out.
It can be about not being able to be involved in activities.
It can be about feeling that most of my friends and family
of my age have passed away –
and I am left!
It can be about not knowing anyone in a group.
It can be about isolation.
It can be about living with confusion and memory loss.
Please take away the loneliness I am feeling.
Help me to feel your presence in a very real way.
Lead members of the church family to visit me when I am
at my lowest.
And enable me to find comfort in the words of Scripture.
In Jesus' name.
Amen.

Feeling sad (the loss of a partner, family member or close friend)

Lord Jesus,
thank you that you understand the feelings of sadness and
loss on the death of a loved one.
The loneliness . . .
The emptiness . . .
The pain . . .
The wondering how to cope without that person.
I need a comforting hug, and the reassurance that I will get
through this.
Please place people around me who care:
to offer comfort;
friends who take the trouble to phone or visit;
those who can offer some practical help;

and someone who really means it when they say, 'Call me any time if you need something.'

Help me in my grief.

Let there be more good days than bad.

Bring me to the point where I can look at photographs and recall the happy memories, rather than the sadness of loss.

Let the knowledge of my faith in you bring hope for the future.

Amen.

Feeling angry (Why me?)

Gracious heavenly Father,

thank you that you are a good listener.

I am feeling angry right now.

It seems so unfair *(talk to God about your situation)*.

I feel so irritated by people who make comments like, 'That's life . . .'

I keep asking the question, 'Why me?'

I really, really struggle to ask the question, 'Why not me?'

I need the freedom to give that anger a voice to express itself in a harmless way.

Please help me to accept my situation; and take away this anger and feeling of injustice.

Grant me a generous and compassionate heart when people make thoughtless or unhelpful comments.

In Jesus' name.

Amen.

Feeling hopeless

Eternal God,

now, in the autumn of life, I have feelings of hopelessness:

I used to love a new project to get my teeth into.

Holidays were something to look forward to.

In my youth I had such plans and ambitions.

Tomorrow was always another day, filled with new opportunities.

Time seems short now:

I feel that there is no point in making long-term plans.

I struggle to feel optimistic.

Thank you for the privilege of serving.

Please grant me purpose in my life still: a worthwhile task to perform.

Help me to feel needed by those around me.

Fill me with hope: not just for eternity, but also for now.

In Jesus' name.

Amen.

What if I want to prepare my own funeral service in advance? Where do I start?

It is not something you have to do, but some people choose to organise their own funeral service in advance. Maybe you feel you would like to reduce the pressure on the family at a time when they will be dealing with practical and emotional issues; or perhaps you have no close family. You might be a person who just likes things to be organised, and feel that the time is right for you to do this. It might be that you have strong feelings about the style and content of your funeral service. You may wish to arrange things with the funeral director as well, or you may just want to organise the service. Whatever your reason, it's absolutely fine.

You might choose to have a friend or family member with you as you plan your funeral service, or you might wish to do it on your own. These are some things for you to consider:

- Where would you like the service to be held?
- Who would you like to take the service?
- Would you like to be buried or cremated?
  - Where would you like to be buried?
  - What would you like to happen with your ashes?
- Choose some favourite hymns: two is probably sufficient for a crematorium, but in a church there will be fewer restrictions on time.

- Select a Bible reading: something that is a favourite, or something that feels particularly appropriate.

- Decide on any additional music, poems, readings, etc. that you would like.

- Are there any members of the family or friends who you would like to do one of the readings? Check that they are willing.

- You could write your own eulogy, or ask someone else to do it.

- You need to decide who you would like to read the eulogy. Check that they are willing.

- Would you like refreshments to be provided after the service?

- Where would you like the gathering after the service to be held?

- What refreshments would you like to be served at this gathering?

- You might need to ring-fence money for the arrangements.

Record your decisions carefully and clearly, and pass them on to someone who can be trusted to make sure that your wishes are carried out (e.g. a minister, family member, friend).

What if the person I am caring for, my friend, my neighbour or a family member wants to prepare their own funeral service in advance? How can I help?

Some people choose to organise their own funeral service for a variety of reasons, and you are in the privileged position of having been chosen to help. The important thing to remember is that it's about what the individual whose service it will be would like. Try not to apply any pressure on them as they make their decisions – even if they ask for advice.

These are some things for you to consider:

- Where would that person like the service to be held?

- Who would they like to take the service?

- Would that person like to be buried or cremated?

    - Where would they like to be buried?

    - What would they like to happen with their ashes?

- Encourage that person to choose some favourite hymns: two is probably sufficient for a crematorium, but in a church there will be fewer restrictions on time.

- Encourage them to select a Bible reading: something that is a favourite, or something that feels particularly appropriate.

- Encourage them to decide on any additional music, poems, readings, etc.

- Are there any members of the family or friends they would like to do one of the readings? Someone will need to check that they are willing.

- That person could write their own eulogy, or ask someone else to do it.

- They will need to decide who they would like to read the eulogy. Someone will need to check that they are willing.

- Would they like refreshments to be provided after the service?

- Where would they like the gathering after the service to be held?

- What refreshments would they like to be served at this gathering?

- They might need to ring-fence money for the arrangements.

Record their decisions carefully and clearly, and pass them on to someone who can be trusted to make sure that their wishes are carried out (e.g. a minister, family member, friend). It might be yourself.

CREATING 'CHURCH' AT HOME SERIES

For people living with
anxiety or depression
1501518

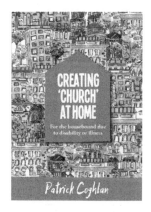

For the housebound due
to disability or illness
1501519

For the elderly
housebound
1501520

Find more books by Patrick
at www.kevinmayhew.com